M000250458

ME, MY PIG AND I

My Life Battling My Inner Food Demon™

Glenn Livingston Ph.D.

CONTENTS

DISCLAIMER: For education only. You are responsible for determining your own nutritional, medical, and psychological needs. If you require assistance with this task you must consult with a licensed physician, nutritionist, psychologist, and/or other professional. No medical, psychological, and/or nutritional advice is offered through this book. Even though the author is a licensed psychologist, he does not offer psychological services, psychological advice and/or psychological counsel in his role as author of this book. In particular, if you have ever been diagnosed with an eating disorder you agree not to create your Food Plan and/or any Food Rules and/or to change your diet in any way without the input and approval of a psychiatrist, psychologist, and licensed dietician. Psy Tech Inc. and/or Never Ever Again, Inc. is only willing to license you the right to utilize this book in the event you agree with these terms. If you do not agree with these terms, please do not read the book, delete it from all electronic devices you own, and/or return it to your place of purchase for a full refund (where applicable). Last, if you follow a link in this book and purchase something on the website on which you land, Psy Tech Inc., and/or Never Ever Again, Inc. may be compensated. While we will never recommend anything we believe is anything other than stellar for your own education and wellbeing, we do not have a neutral position, so you are advised to do your own due diligence before purchase.

© Psy Tech Inc. and Never Ever Again, Inc. All Rights Reserved

INTRODUCTION

Weird Things I Did That Make This Book Worth Reading

If you've purchased this book, odds are good you know who I am, and value the unusual perspective I have on overeating. But did you know the following about me?

➤ I taught marketing to over 30,000 entrepreneurs, built a coach training organization which competed on the world stage, had a thriving child and family therapy practice just outside NYC, headed two consulting companies which sold $30,000,000+ to Fortune 500 firms *(many in the food industry)*, and both built and sold a digital marketing agency.

➤ I regret the work I did for Big Food. I was on the WRONG side of the war and it was a waste of my time, energy, and talent. It did, however, give me an insider's view, which helped me understand the social epidemic of overeating in a way others can't see.

➤ Pretty much everyone in my family is a psychotherapist. My mom, dad, sister, step-dad, step-mom, brother-in-law, grandma, two of my cousins, my aunts, great uncle, his wife, my ex-wife, and several more. This had a deep impact on my perspective and ability to formulate Never Binge Again. *(Try saying "Dr. Livingston I Presume" more than once if you're feeling lucky!)*

➤ I was absolutely miserable with food for 30 years. There

was a time I was almost 280 pounds, compulsively ate sugar out of the garbage, had a slew doctors screaming I was going to die, and was $700,000 in debt. I was fat, sick, and broke, but I could've just been broke. If you have six problems and you overeat, you'll have seven problems! This was NOT the most traumatic period of my life though, and NOT worth binging over.

➤ Finally, you might also know I've once again been through a LOT of trauma in the past few years. A painful divorce. My mother's death. Losing my rescue dog of 14 years whom I loved more than I knew you could love another living soul. Moving four times, including twice across the country by myself. Having to exit the coach training organization I'd worked so hard to build because it was intimately entangled with my ex-wife. Falling head over heels in love and having my heart handed back to me in a vice. But through these more recent traumas I did NOT lose control of my eating, because in my early 40s I discovered the very strange, but incredibly effective way to control it which became Never Binge Again.

THIS book, "Me, My Pig, and I" tells the rest of the story, so you can better leverage the insights and power of "Never Binge Again."

One Last Thing Before We Start

I didn't have to solve my emotional issues to get better. It was perfectly possible to stop overeating by isolating, ignoring, and disempowering the voice of justification inside my head (the "Pig") which kept convincing me to break my best laid dietary plans.

But it can still be tempting to conclude the personal traumas and triumphs you'll read about "caused" my binge eating, and that it wasn't until I solved them that I was able to stop. To disavow you of THAT notion, let me tell you right here and now that, to this day, I have NOT completely solved all of my childhood traumas, nor has anyone else for that matter. As I write this, even though my life is MUCH grander than I ever expected it would be, and even though I am SO much better than I was 40 years ago, in many ways I'm still neurotic. I still find myself worried about things which will probably never happen...but that does NOT stop me from being 100% confident I Will Never Binge Again!

OK! Let's get started...

CHAPTER 1: BORN HUNGRY!

The story which surrounds a person's birth is meaningful. You can't ever know if it's accurate, but it still represents something about the dynamic in which your parents and other significant figures raised you. After all, this is the way they chose to remember meeting you.

The very first thing my mother *(Joyce Livingston http:// www.neverbingeagain.com/images/JoyceLivingstonPretty.jpg)* told me when I asked her about my birth was that she MUCH preferred when I was inside her womb to after I was born. "At least then I always knew where you were Glenn!" she joked. After that, she was constantly worried I was unsafe and/or making trouble... which I admittedly was.

It's funny, but also a clear manifestation of Mom's anxious makeup. Mom worried about everything, and it unfortunately rubbed off on me. The world became a MUCH scarier place than it needed to be. Though years of therapy, journaling, and self-reflection I've mostly managed to shed this perspective, but at times irrational anxiety still haunts me:

> ➤ "I am an old man and have known a great many troubles, but most of them never happened. Worrying is like paying a debt you don't owe. I have spent most of my life worrying about things that have never happened. Drag your thoughts away from your troubles... by the ears, by the heels, or any other way you can manage it." – Mark Twain

Ditto that!

Unfortunately, the anxious nature Mom gifted me left me very conflict averse. I've spent way too much of my energy seeking stability and security, to the detriment of my most significant pursuits.

In more recent years I've undertaken to conquer neurotic worries in the same way I conquered binge eating—using my head to intellectually figure out what behavior is reasonable, sketching out clear rules to define those behaviors, and then assuming every other thought and feeling (*all the doubt and insecurity*) is "Pig Squeal"... nothing more than the neurological misfiring of my reptilian brain.

For example, I LOVE swimming in the ocean and recently moved to the beach. There's something about the gentle—*and sometimes not so gentle*—motion of the waves lifting me up and putting me back down I find simultaneously refreshing and soothing. Incredibly so.

But I also live not so far from the shark attack capital of the world, and because of this, it took me at least a month to get into the water past my ankles. When I applied reason to assess the risk, however, I realized it was extremely silly for me to walk to the beach and not go in the water, despite living in world-record shark attack territory. Why? *(Data from https://www.floridamuseum.ufl.edu/shark-attacks/odds/compare-risk/death/)*

> The risk of dying from a SHARK ATTACK in your lifetime is **1 in 3,748,067**

> The lifetime odds of being killed by a LIGHTENING STRIKE are 1 in 79,746

> The lifetime odds of DROWNING are 1 in 1,134

> The lifetime odds of dying in a CAR ACCIDENT are 1 in

84

> The odds of dying of the FLU anytime during your lifetime are 1 in 63

> The lifetime odds of dying of HEART DISEASE are 1 in 5!

So, even though I AM quite delicious, I'm 47 times more likely to be killed by lightening than eaten by a shark, 3,305 times more likely to drown, 44,620 times more likely to be killed in a car accident, 59,493 times more likely to die of flu, and 749,613 times more likely to die of heart disease...

But in our culture, media pays a lot more attention to very rare events, and our fear response is much more centered around them. There's even a theory that suggests if we were to focus our fear on the everyday, common things required for living (*e.g. like driving*) and/or economic growth (*e.g. eating industrially manufactured foods*) then society as we know it couldn't function. We therefore all walk around frightened of shark attacks and terrorists, when what we should REALLY be frightened of are potato chips, pizza, flu germs, and cars! The truth is, I'm infinitely more likely to get killed crossing the street on the way to the beach than to be eaten by a shark.

Plus, becoming a shark's dinner would be a pretty bad-ass way to go. Can't you just see everyone talking about it at the funeral? "How did he go? Got eaten by a shark! Plus, the dude helped millions of people with binge eating. Dr. Livingston sure was one bad-ass psychologist!" Come to think of it, if I ever do get eaten by a shark can someone please ensure this quote gets inscribed on my tombstone?

The point is, I'm a strong swimmer and it's just plain stupid to avoid going in the ocean.

I therefore researched how to minimize shark attraction: Don't swim at dusk or dawn. Don't wear brightly contrasting colors. Don't go in the water with a fresh, oozing wound and a big sign that says "Hey sharks! Here's dinner!" Then I made a rule for myself to swim 100 yards from shore three days per week and stay there for fifteen minutes. I not only feel incredibly refreshed when I come out, but ready to face all my other unreasonable fears too...

Like the fear of being too deprived if I give up some not-so-good-for-me food treat, the fear of going bankrupt, of being called a fraud, and/or never finding love again. These fears all seem miniscule after I've taunted Jaws for a while with my yummy legs. *(Actually, fun fact, sharks prefer fatty meals like seals, so staying trim protects me too...but you get the point.)*

The formula is (1) Seek out information to quantify the risk; (2) Research how to minimize it; (3) Decide on a realistic risk worth taking; (4) Define a clear behavioral plan, articulated in exquisitely clear language; (5) Decide any thought which suggests you shouldn't execute the plan is Squeal.

I wish I'd known this was possible 40 years ago!

Back to my embryonic years, Mom ate almost nothing besides fatty lamb chops and pistachio-mint chocolate chip ice cream while she was pregnant with me. Must've gotten that advice from all the books she read on how to create a binge eater. All kidding aside, I absolutely adored my mother, but the type of nutrition she chose while we shared the same blood MUST have had an impact. I must've become used to all the sugar, fat, and salt as my heart, lungs, muscles, digestive system, and brain were first developing. This was my earliest physical experience. As psychologists we now know that babies DO learn in the womb. It had to have planted some seeds.

What stories are there about what YOUR mom ate while she was pregnant with you? How might that have affected you to this day?

Anyway, I was *supposed* to be born on August 21st, 1964, which was also *Mom's* birthday. She was VERY excited about sharing her special day with me, but, because I was so fiercely independent, I refused and waited to claim August 26th for my own.

My parents lived just outside of Washington D.C. at the time, and Dad was a captain stationed at Water Reed Army Hospital. He was also a psychologist and hypnotist working with PTSD victims from Viet Nam. When dad got the news I was to be born, he was on his way back to the hospital, eating peanuts in the car. Shells in hand, he drove smack into the back of a truck. Thankfully, he wasn't hurt.

The way Mom recounts the story there was a raging hurricane that day. But when I researched the historical weather archives for August 26th, 1964, I found no such event. In fact, there was virtually NO precipitation! There was, however, a very heavy tropical storm named "Cleo" which hit about a week later. 5.80" of rain fell one hundred seventy miles to the west of Washington D.C. on September 1st, 1964.

There must've been *storm warnings* around my birthday, so I'm guessing Mom was just anxious and overreacting, like she always did. Then the story morphed into a hurricane as she told it repeatedly over the years, the way any good fish story does. The discrepancy makes me wonder how many other gross exaggerations I believed my whole life. Did she really date the advertising executive who invented the slogan "Betcha can't eat just one" for example? She said so, and I set out to prove him right.

My birth itself was uneventful, and Glenn Scott Livingston came into the world at 7:21 am on 8/26/1964, kicking ass, taking names, and ready to eat. 24" tall, 7 pounds 11 ounces, I was a force to be reckoned with! *(NEW BORN: http:// www.neverbingeagain.com/images/GlennNewBorn1964.jpg , ABOUT NINE MONTHS: http://www.neverbingeagain.com/images/ GlennAbout9Months.jpg)*

From the very beginning I was difficult to feed. I had colic, and Mom says I just cried and screamed all the time until I passed out.

It's very interesting the mark such early experiences can leave on both mother and son. Until her dying day Mom panicked about feeding me. For example, I remember walking into her kitchen in 2017 during her final weeks on the planet. She was making eggs for her husband, and she got a horrendous look on her face when she saw me. "Oh my God! Oh my God! What can I feed you Glenn!?" Then, with her bare hands, she accidentally grabbed the hot frying pan by the wrong end and burned herself.

Thankfully she wasn't injured too badly. When the smoke cleared and we'd attended to her physical needs, I realized her reaction was very strange indeed. Mom knew *exactly* what I could eat. In fact, she'd already prepared her house beautifully for my visit. There was more healthy, substantial, and nourishing food than any man could possibly need for a five-day stay. Much more than I kept for myself in my own home. I could've eaten like a king for weeks and felt good about it. But mom was absolutely terrified of seeing me in the kitchen.

In fact, Mom was very frightened of being a Mom in general, especially when I was first born. It was equally clear she loved and adored me, but she was frightened ALL the time. Why? Only Mom knows for sure, but I can speculate...

In the mid 60's Vietnam was heating up, and the government was talking about sending Dad overseas to the war zone. By the time I was one year old, Mom was trying to get pregnant again, and she must've feared winding up as an army widow with two young children and no way to support them. She'd been an English teacher in an inner city junior high school for very low pay before she got pregnant. She reportedly spent more than her salary on extra supplies for the kids. Plus, remember, this was 1965 and opportunities for young women were nothing like they are today.

Also, Mom's world had really fallen apart just before I was born.

Glenn Livingston

Although I didn't know this until I was in my early twenties, Mom's father *("Pa Mike" to me)* had just gotten out of prison, and he was guilty as sin. He'd been doing very bad things.

Mom had always idolized and adored her dad. In fact, he, my great-grandmother Lena, and her gay next-door neighbor "Charlie" were her only salvations in childhood. She'd grown up with a crazy mother *("Ma Pearl")* who was always terrified of a Japanese invasion. "The Japs are coming!", "The Japs are on the balcony!", my grandmother would say with sheer terror in my mother's youth.

My understanding is that Ma Pearl beat mom regularly, though Mom only hinted at it and hated talking about those things. And great-grandma Lena, whom I never met, was a schizophrenic immigrant who beat Ma Pearl in turn, but absolutely adored my mother.

Then, well, I didn't come with an instruction book, and Mom's parents didn't prepare her very well for motherhood. Plus, dad worked a lot as an army psychologist, so Mom was mostly on her own.

My earliest feeding experiences were therefore a real ordeal. I've seen videos of Mom bottle-feeding me, and what's striking is, it looks like I'm trying to get AWAY from the bottle. The formula is oozing out of my mouth and it appears I must've been uncomfortably full. When I looked at the videos as an adult I thought "Mom, that baby doesn't need any more food, he just needs a hug!"

At the same time, you've never seen more love on a woman's face than the way she looked at me. I'm SURE that's where I learned my first lesson in overeating "Uncomfortably Full = Love." Is it any wonder I repeated that experience again and again throughout life?

What are the earliest stories about feeding you as an infant? What might you take away from them?

10

You can see a little video here of Mom and I during her last few months of life if you're curious. She was just about to go for chemotherapy. I think she'd made peace with the idea it was going to kill her. To that point Mom had suffered two heart attacks, two strokes, three falls down the stairs, and three bouts of cancer. She was ready to go, and I have very little doubt the doctors obliged with a way for her to do so.

Rest in Peace mom. You did your very best and I can eat normally now. Life is good. There are people who love me. I have meaningful work and good friends. And I'm not done yet Mom, there's a grand adventure yet to come. I'm OK now and I love you.

Before you read further, you might like to take a few moments to jot down what you remember about your own birth story. Don't worry about understanding it, just write it down. You'll thank me for the insights it provides you through the years.

There aren't many stories about Dad (http://www.neverbingeagain.com/images/ DadCaptainChubby.JPG) during my first year on the planet. He was working very hard at his job. There are a bunch of pictures of him holding me and playing with me. He was always a kind of warm, fuzzy presence in my life. He was chubby in those early years but thin later. Now he's 81 years old and exercises two hours per day! I'm so proud of him.

CHAPTER 2: KEEP EATING – MY YUMMY PRESCHOOL YEARS

Here are a few pictures of me during this phase for reference:

http://www.neverbingeagain.com/images/ThreeYearOldGlenn.jpg

http://www.neverbingeagain.com/images/Mom-Funky-Glasses-Glenn-Two.jpg

http://www.neverbingeagain.com/images/KidsLoveMomma.jpg

Go Get Your Bosco Glenn

If you've listened to any of my radio show interviews, you probably know the chocolate Bosco story. In a nutshell, mom was overwhelmed, depressed, and anxious when I was a toddler, and didn't always have the wherewithal to feed me or love me when I came to her. So she kept a big bottle of Bosco chocolate syrup in a refrigerator on the floor, and at those moments she'd say "Go get your Bosco Glenn!" I'd cheerfully oblige, run *(or crawl)* to the refrigerator, take out the bottle, open the cap, and suck on it while I sunk into a chocolate sugar coma.

That's probably the match which struck the fire of my chocolate addiction but having this insight did NOT solve the problem. In fact, it made it worse, because it gave my inner-destructive-food voice (my "Pig") justification: "Oooooooh, Glenn, our Mama didn't love us, you got that right! She left a great big chocolate sized hole in our hearts. And until we can find the love of our life and fill up that hole with what we really need, we'll just have to keep binging on chocolate. Let's go get more right fricking now!! Please can we? PLEAZZZ!!"

This was one of the critical insights which, in my early 40s, helped me to understand I needed to stop trying to love myself thin and/or nurture my inner wounded child. Instead, I needed to act like an alpha wolf being challenged for leadership by a lesser member of the pack (my reptilian brain). "Get back in line or I'll kill you" was a much more effective attitude. So sad nobody taught me that in 1969. Oh well, I guess that's why they say "youth is wasted on the young."

I cover the method which worked to end my food addiction in Never Binge Again. In *this* book my job is to give you more insight into how it developed. Towards that end, let's talk about a wide variety of early childhood incidents which illustrate the course of the addiction.

Sleeping in the Mushrooms

I've always loved mushrooms. I used to literally beg for them from the time I was only one year old. When my parents took me out to eat, they'd get the chef to prepare a whole plate full of mushrooms. I'm guessing in marinara sauce because Mom and Dad had a penchant for Italian food.

Anyway, one time my parents were busy talking to each other at the restaurant without watching me, so I decided to eat the mushrooms doggy style, with my face buried in the plate. Because hey, I'm not stupid – I know an opportunity when I see it! Anyway, before they knew it, I was asleep with my face IN the mushrooms.

Mom always enjoyed telling that story.

It's a good metaphor for how I spent a good part of my life, with my face buried in delicious food instead of participating in conversation, engaged with other people, and grabbing life by the balls. I was always more interested in food opportunities than people opportunities. Food addiction keeps your face buried in the mushrooms.

Later in life, when I recovered, I learned to "wake myself up" at the moment of impulse by saying *"Get your face out of the mushrooms and go talk to someone Glenn!"*

Do you have your own iconic "mushroom" story? When did you first start burying your face in food? What mantra or pithy saying can you derive to remind you not to do that when you catch yourself?

Sharing Candy with Amy

At three years old I had my first girlfriend, Amy. She was a gorgeous red head, and her mother had taken her to the set of Sesame Street. I was insanely jealous! And the combination of her hair, that freckled face, and all the Big Bird talk was too much for me to resist.

I always asked for extra Tootsie Pops and chocolate milk for Amy whenever Mom gave me some, and she'd praise me for remembering. Sometimes I'd bring Amy other candy, milkshakes, and pizza. Mom thought that was adorable. Yes indeed, when you love someone, you feed them excess sugar, starch, and fat. Is it any wonder that in my house I was constantly bathed in it? A powerful life lesson from 1967.

What did you learn about how to love someone with food in your earliest years? Can you come up with a specific story?

Tootsie Pops

"How many licks does it take to get to the center of a tootsie pop? The world may never know!"

Such was the slogan uttered by the Tootsie Pop Owl on the

airwaves in the late 1960s. He demonstrated a few licks before caving and biting through to the Tootsie Roll center. He could NEVER resist biting long enough to find out. I, on the other hand, was very determined, and constantly begged my mother for more pops to conduct experiments. My first lesson in the power of Big Food advertising!

I never did figure it out, but a group of engineering students at Purdue University built a licking machine to do the job. Turns out the answer was 364. Then a University of Michigan student got a different answer from his machine – 411. A group of human volunteers at Swarthmore Junior High School came to a much different conclusion – 144 licks.

I guess we really will never know!

During these same years I discovered "Honeycomb's big! Yeah yeah yeah", "Lucky Charms" were magically delicious, "Frosted Flakes" were grrrrrrrrrrrrrrrreeeeeeeeeeeeeeat, "Coca Cola" was the real thing, and Double Mint Gum doubled your pleasure and doubled your fun.

The Big Food and Big Advertising programming machine went to work on my mind early. Odds are, it did on yours too!

A Constant Bath of Sugar, Starch, and Fat

Sugar, starch, and fat was constantly available in my house from the time I was old enough to reach the cabinets and the refrigerator door. I'd eat whole boxes of sugary cereal in one sitting–Cocoa Puffs, Frosted Flakes, Sugar Pops, Honey Comb, Frankenberry, Lucky Charms, and more. When I was just a little older, I'd graduate to whole boxes of chocolate fudge PopTarts every single morning.

In the refrigerator you could always find cream cheese and bagels, lox, Jarlsberg cheese, potter's cheese, chopped liver, whole chickens *(with the fatty skin),* and often left-over lamb, pizza, and meatloaf.

Every weekend my grandparents *(Mom's parents)* would visit with a few boxes of donuts. I especially looked forward to those visits and would eat most of them myself. Ma Pearl and Pa Mike would also bring all sorts of fun toys. Spirograph, Etch A Sketch, Chutes and Ladders, etc.

When I was a little older, my parents started ordering an entire case of Coca Cola each week. I guess they thought we were drinking it, which makes it pretty darn scary they kept placing the orders...

The thing of it is though, my sister and I were NOT drinking the soda. Instead, as soon as we found out it made a great noise when you poured it on the carpet, we found a place behind her bed where my parents wouldn't check, and we'd just pour can after can on the rug when nobody was watching.

Yes, we were very disturbed children. I'm sorry Momma!

Anyway, I'm not sure if I even knew what a vegetable was until I was college. I WISH I were exaggerating for dramatic effect but I'm not. Maybe we had creamed spinach occasionally, or some corn. I just barely remember eating any fruit either.

Fun = food. Love = food. Life = food.

Sugar, starch, fat.

That's what I learned at an early age in the 1960s.

The Brown Chair

In my earliest years, my mother smacked me across the face when I did something wrong. As a psychologist, this bothered my father to no end, so he created a special chair for me to sit in for "time outs" instead. The "Brown Chair."

What I remember about the brown chair, which I can see in my mind as if it were yesterday, was that I didn't really mind being sent to it. In fact, I rather enjoyed it. See, the Brown Chair was in the middle of all the action in the living room where everyone hung out. It was comfortable. Nobody bothered me there. I could breathe and relax for a bit rather than getting all caught up in wanting this toy or that, being upset about not getting a fourth jelly donut from the table, etc.

Plus, once the Brown Chair was introduced, I never got hit again. Not that I specifically remember being hit, but I know Mom and Dad are telling the truth because even now I have that awful feeling in my eyes whenever someone gets very angry with me. And Mom profusely apologized for it in later years.

Anyway...

I ABSOLUTELY LOVED BEING SENT TO THE BROWN CHAIR. It was kind of like a worker in a corporate office being told "Go take a day at the beach as punishment for your behavior." OK, cool. I'll do it! Should I get a massage on the corporate dime on the way back? I want to take my punishment like a man, you know.

Now, here's an even stranger thing...

From the above dynamics you'd THINK I would've wound up behaving worse to get sent to the Brown Chair. But I didn't. It served its purpose and gradually I got sent to the brown chair less and less often...

Until—*and I DO remember this part clear as day*—I asked Mom if I could just go to the brown chair when I *wanted* to instead of having to do something bad first. And that's exactly what happened. I just went and hung out on the brown chair whenever I wanted a break. I LOVED it.

The brown chair taught me how to take time outs when I needed them. Instead of getting all caught up in the action of the moment—*sometimes even when that action involved sugar, fat,*

17

and starch!—I could just go take a breather.

The brown chair is one thing my parents did right. Really, it was a miracle, and I wish they'd saved the chair as we moved from place to place. I'd love to have it now, or at least a picture as a reminder.

It wasn't until my mid-30s that I discovered I could use NATURE as my modern-day brown chair. It's sad, but I had to be all grown up before I realized I could prevent a binge by indulging in a "time out" by the water, in the woods, or the mountains.

Which brings me to an important point...

Sometimes I think my reaction to nature is very extreme. I wonder if I'm just not like other people. I think most people see nature as something "really nice." They feel a little better when they can integrate some time outdoors into their lives a few times each month. To them, it's a luxurious, "once in a while" indulgence. But to me, it's something I simply can't live without, like oxygen. I feel like I'm going to wither and die if I don't get outside every day for at least a half hour, preferably more.

When I stand and look at the sunrise on the beach, I feel overwhelmed, almost to tears. When I reach the top of a mountain after a long hike, I get a deep sense of meaning and purpose inside my soul. Even when I open my balcony door at night to breath in the cool ocean breeze, I feel like I've died and gone to heaven, like something is cleansing me at the deepest level.

In fact, without nature, life almost feels pointless. Which is not to say I don't crave deep connection to people, romantic love, friendships, and other types of adventures. Goodness knows I've made every effort to fill my life in this way *...some very successful, some not so much!* But in the end, a big part of my struggle to overcome binge eating had to do with coming to terms with the fact I ABSOLUTELY <u>REQUIRE</u> NATURE in a society that's willing to sacrifice it for the bottom line.

Overeating takes me out of the present moment and deprives me of the ability to embrace the outdoors with all the splendor it has to offer. I don't think we were meant to live between four walls, staring at computer screens, trying to make electrons float into our bank accounts. At least I wasn't. And I had to fight my way through the general population's relegation of nature to a "nice to have" vs. "must have" status in order to find the motivation.

Every day I binge ate was a day I couldn't let nature nourish me. But I eventually learned I could dominate my urges if I nourished my body with healthy food and prioritized my "time outs" outdoors.

I wish we lived in a world where everyone saw nature like oxygen, not just something you indulged in occasionally when there was enough cash in your wallet. In the meantime, I've learned to just accept this about myself. I can't live without nature any more than I could live without oxygen and water. If that makes me a weirdo, so be it. It's my Brown Chair for life.

What's your Brown Chair?

Enter the Sister

Womb Time

When I was approximately two years old my dad put my sister into Mom's uterus. Mom started really showing a few months before my birthday, and Laurie Sue Livingston came into the world in November of 1966 with a smile on her face, pigtails on her head, and trouble-making in her eyes. My sister says to call her "Laura" now because she's all grown up with kids of her own, and she's also a doctor and stuff, but she'll always be Laurie to me!

➢ Laurie and I when we were kids: http://
www.neverbingeagain.com/images/GlennAndLaurieLittle.JPG

➤ Laurie now: http://www.neverbingeagain.com/images/ SissyGlassesSeptember2018.jpg

I talked to Laurie all the time when she lived in Mom's tummy. I kept her updated on my favorite TV shows...mostly The Banana Splits, Underdog, and Felix the Cat. I also told her about all the yummy treats I was going to feed her when she came out, and how much fun we were going to have eating and playing together. I urged her to hurry up and get out. I thought it was just plain stupid that she was spending so much time in my mother's stomach when it was so much more fun in the world.

Turns out Laurie was much more than an eating buddy though. We played all sorts of games together. Also, I was the one who taught her how to talk because I understood what she was saying way before my parents did. I specifically remember teaching her how to say "Thank you", which to this day still sounds like "Fang you" to me when she says it because that's how it first came out.

Laurie had a great imagination and was TONS of fun. We were best buddies, and still are. We speak every day. *(We don't live in the same city.)*

But apparently, I wasn't so happy about my darling little sister the first few weeks after she was born. I kept asking when Mom was going bring her back to the hospital, or if she could just put Laurie back in her tummy where she belonged. Absent that, I wanted to know why she and Dad didn't just throw her out the car window. But I guess I must've gotten used to Laurie as Mom says that phase was relatively short lived. I went back to being happy about the whole sister thing pretty quickly.

The Doggy Game

One of my favorite memories in Laurie's earliest years was playing "The Doggy Game." I was a magic professor and she was my dog slave.

That's it...

That's the whole game.

Other than the occasional "sit" and "stay", mostly it meant she had to go fetch me Pop-Tarts. When she got a little older, Laurie was no longer willing to play. Now she's not even willing to admit it ever happened, but it did!

I never quite got used to not having a dog-slave to fetch my junk, but I don't blame her. It was fun while it lasted.

The Doggy Game is the earliest representation I can recall that documents my previous obsession with finding the most calories for the least effort. In recent years I've crystalized it into a mantra I use whenever I find myself feeling lazy about shopping and preparing healthy food for myself: "Stop Playing the Doggy Game, Glenn!" By the way, I find for every hour I put into shopping, preparing, and other healthy-food support activities, I get another three or four hours of productivity that I would've lost by eating poorly. This mantra has been very useful.

Is there an early childhood memory which might represent your obsession with food in a similar way? Or perhaps some way you learned to be lazy about doing the work necessary to support your health goals? Can you turn this into a concise mantra you can repeat to yourself each day, especially at the moment of impulse?

"I Want the Gerbils to Go Back in Their Cage"

Another favorite memory is from when I was four and Laurie was two. She woke us all up saying "I want the gerbils to go back in their cage!" Apparently, she'd let our little pets out to play without thinking about the consequences. We spent all night chasing them around the apartment and got to skip school the next day. Thanks for the memory sis.

Of course, this is yet another iconic representation about how both Laurie and I got rewarded for doing the wrong things as children. But I'm not sure Mom and Dad had any choice on this one.

Here's a takeaway for you regarding eating healthy…

Don't let your Pig out of it's Cage or it'll do it's best to run around the house and keep you up all night… and you'll have to go to school/work anyway.

"I Want My Face Back!"

Then there was Laurie's first haircut. Mom took us both to my barber together when I'd been used to going alone. He was dumbfounded by how much we looked alike:

"Oh my goodness, she has his face!" he said.

I did NOT like this _at all_. I started screaming…

"I WANT MY FACE BACK! GIVE ME MY FACE BACK!! MOMMY!!! LAURIE TOOK MY FACE AND SHE WON'T GIVE IT BACK! MOOO-OOOMMMMMMY!!!"

See? I wasn't necessarily Ph.D. material from the get-go, but I guess all's well that ends well!

Laurie is my only sibling, and for the first 50 years of my life I thought of her as my "little sister" to love and protect. But more recently, as I was getting divorced, she came through for me in a big way. I'd never stopped to think she'd been a psychologist for 25 years herself! Laurie started calling me every day and knew just what to say. I was amazed and have had a newfound respect for her ever since. I don't know how I would've made it without her.

Even this memory proved useful to me. "Nobody took your face Glenn!" is a mantra I use when I find myself getting emotionally worked up about things for no reason. And that's one less thing my Pig can use to try and convince me to binge!

You might wish to pause for a moment to think of a childhood memory which represents how you can get worked up for no reason. Then turn it into a mantra to snap you back into your more rational, adult self.

Sugar as a Reward System

Sugar was not only constantly available in my earliest years, but special forms of it were used as a reward for behaving and/or performing well. For example, whenever we got a 100% cavity free checkup at the dentist Mom would take us for chocolate milkshakes. Kind of defeats the purpose, I know, but that's how things were in the Livingston household.

On weekends, if we were good, Pa Mike would take us to Burger King for whoppers, fries, and milkshakes. Later, when I decided to stop eating animals, sugar, and fried food, I found it very difficult to shake the Burger King addiction. Who'd want to let go of those memories?

The pivotal moment for me was when I realized I didn't have to! The happy moments driving in the car, sitting across from my grandfather while he smiled and entertained us, laughing with my sister... there was NO reason to throw out the baby with the bathwater. I only needed to throw out the "food."

In fact, I could consciously bathe in all the good feelings associated with these memories by journaling about them, looking for pictures from my past, finding pictures in magazines which reminded me of those experiences and creating a collage, etc.

You might want to pause here and try to recall one happy memory from your childhood which is associated with "Slop." How can you hold onto all the good memories and feelings WITHOUT the poisonous "food" your Pig associates with them?

The Dad

Dad's Earliest Years

Martin Edward Sandleman was born in 1938 in Brooklyn, NY, the son of Esther and George Sandleman. Grandpa George died when my father was only 4 years old, the defining event of dad's childhood. I never met my grandfather.

Shortly thereafter Esther took dad to live at her mother's house with several of dad's uncles, aunts, and their families. Dad was in heaven. Little Martin Sandleman was loved and adored by everyone in that house and there's always a warmth in his voice when he speaks of it.

Grandma Esther Remarries

When dad was approximately nine years old his mother remarried a wealthy man named Jack Livingston (*where my last name comes from*), and both she and dad moved to his household where Jack was already raising two children. Dad never felt accepted there and spent a relatively unhappy second half of his childhood as a very rebellious adolescent.

It's hard to get many memories out of dad about those troubled times, except that he and a friend did a little bullying around the neighborhood. You'd never know it from the way he is now —he's become the sweetest old man! He's also in incredible shape for an 81-year-old guy. He plays competitive tennis and/or goes to the gym for two hours each day. He also still works 20 to 30 hours per week. (*Psychologists almost never retire.*)

As you'll see later in my story, Dad and I weren't super close while I was married—but we connected on a much deeper level shortly after Mom died and have been making up for lost time ever since. My biggest regret in life is the distance I allowed to grow between us.

Dad Meets Mom

Marty met my mom (Joyce) in 1952 when he was only 14 and

she was only 12. They exclusively dated from that point on, and were married in 1958, just a few months before my Dad's twentieth birthday. Because they were SO young, people constantly told them it was only "puppy love" and they'd never make it.

I think dad's persistent willingness to pursue things against the odds, and despite what everyone else said, was part of what imbued the courage in me to do so myself. I can't imagine I ever would've found such a counter-culture way to overcome overeating *(and relentlessly pursued perfecting it)* if there hadn't been some model of success against common beliefs in my past. Indeed, it was a part of my parents' initial bond – without which my creation would never have occurred!

Looking back on your childhood, who was the single most positive influence in your life? Was there some way they gave you courage to pursue off-beat solutions to seemingly impossible problems? Take a moment and crystalize the memory. You might want to write it down.

Dad Puts Baby Glenn in Mom's Uterus

Six years later, my Dad had his doctorate and a steady job as a captain in the army, so they could make the decision to bring baby Glenn into the world. I often wonder what army policies had to do with the timing of this decision, since it was smack in the middle of the era when Viet Nam was heating up, and the government was less likely to send captains overseas if they had a child. *(Even less likely for two child families).*

Regardless, the decision was made.

The odds are pretty good, if you do the math, that I was conceived on or around the day JFK was shot. I know both mom and dad had been filled with hope about JFK's Presidency, so I like to imagine they were taking solace in one another on the night I decided to make myself comfy in Mom's uterus.

Regardless of whether this is true or not, I've always had the sense I was a product of love. I was WANTED.

Not everyone is this lucky. It's OK if you don't feel like this. I've worked with hundreds of patients who didn't feel they were a product of love in their family. It's only important you identify, to the best of your ability, what was going on in your parents' lives which might've made it difficult for them to give you the love you needed. It's important you realize, if you didn't get the love you needed—and many people do NOT—it wasn't because of you.

Children are lovable by nature. It's a birthright. If you lived and breathed, you WERE lovable.

It's also important to remember you can GIVE other people the love you didn't get. Indeed, this is perhaps the only way I've ever found for people to heal from feeling unwanted and/or unloved. Search yourself for all you needed but were deprived of in your childhood, then resolve to give that to others. As you watch them transform, you will transform yourself. "Be the person you needed when you were younger" - Ayesha Siddiqi.

Once people get this idea at the deepest level, I find they can heal ANYTHING in their life. And while I WAS deeply loved by both my parents, they also made a million and one mistakes which damaged me. It's only through this concept that I've been able to heal that damage.

Who and what did you need when you were younger? How can you give that to others? Write it down in detail. Ask yourself what single behavior and/or thought you must engage in each day to be the person you needed when you were younger. It might be the most important thing you ever do.

Dad Was the Voice of Health in Our Household

From the earliest days, Dad was always the voice of healthy reason in our household. He was heavy himself in my preschool days, but exercise and sports were always very important to him.

I recall my sister, mother, and I would NEVER eat too much crap in front of him. But as soon as we were alone with mom, out came the junk.

I don't necessarily agree with everything my Dad thought was healthy *(or does to this day)*, but I do highly respect him for trying to hold that line, and for HAVING a line in the first place. It was genuinely important to him that our family was raised to value health, and I think without his values I very well could've been 500 pounds. I probably would've written a book called "Binge Some More" instead of "Never Binge Again." I guess it wouldn't've been too popular, but it would've been fun to write. I could've sat around with all my chubby friends drinking beer, eating chips, and talking about the recipes. Oh well, maybe in another life.

In all seriousness, Dad, coupled with my grandfather, was a driving force for health in my life. I remember how excited he'd get whenever we'd get a treadmill or some other new piece of gym equipment for the house. "The family is going to be so much healthier now" I recall him saying. I also remember how much he and Pa Mike enjoyed anything outdoors or in the pool. I remember his constant focus on whether any given food was "fattening" or not. I remember his interest in various exercise regimens. I remember how he always chose healthy, active vacation spots.

I imagine this focus came from his memories of his father before he died. When I was little, Dad always seemed very attached to his father's image, and I guess all he had to go on later were the memories of his father's athleticism. *(George, my grandfather, had been a gym teacher in a local high school before he died of a kidney disease.)*

Sometimes you can trace values back several generations. Knowing what was important to your ancestors can provide motivation and direction for your life. In part, my motivation to be a health leader in the world started with my grandfather's decision to become a gym teacher, even though I never met him! "Honor your ancestors by thriving!"

Where does health motivation come from in your family tree? It's worth a few minutes to consider. *(Note: I did a great podcast interview on the topic of using the stories of your ancestors' suffering to push you forward in life. Listen here: https://www.neverbingeagain.com/TheBlog/recorded-sessions/honor-your-ancestors-by-thriving-not-binging/)*

Some Negative Food Influence from Poppa

Of course, some of my food obsession came from Dad too. He loved to go out to dinner, and as the first upwardly mobile person in his family, he made sure we did so frequently. Even then, we always talked about what we were ordering and whether it was fattening. *(There were no such conversations when we were alone with Mom).*

Eating out frequently was a mixed blessing. On the one hand, I was always aware how lucky I was to be in a prosperous, upper-middle-class family. I had friends from the "other side of the tracks" who made sure I knew! On the other hand, it became normal to bathe my blood stream even further in all the excess sugar, starch, fat, and salt in restaurants, and I associated even more good times and loving memories with these dinners.

When we are out, my parents also NEVER fought like they did at other times, so eating at restaurants became further romanticized as something "magical."

Last, dad loved the fatty part of the steak, and it always bothered me to watch him devour it. I can still remember the fat dripping down his face. I wound up with an aversion to unhealthy fats because of this, so in an odd way I owe him a debt of thanks on this point. Later, my sister picked up on how much this bothered me and started delighting in eating plain sticks of butter in front of me.

Isn't family great?

By the way, this is a very mild example of how adversity in childhood can create strength in adulthood. Our culture tends to make us believe every trauma results only in a wound—but it can result in a character strength too.

Do you have any negative food memories which make it easier for you to avoid unhealthy foods today?

Dad Worked a Lot

I don't remember seeing Dad too much during my preschool years. He was working at the army base and the hospital. But my memories of him when he *was* around are all positive. In fact, I recall Mom being happiest when Dad was home, and somewhat unstable *(depressed, anxious, and prone to short fits of irrational anger)* when he wasn't.

As I mentioned in the brown chair section, mom would sometimes hit me in the face during her bouts of severe anxiety and depression, exacerbating my fear of the world. She'd never do this when my father was there. So, having Dad around always felt very safe, and because of this I think I very strongly identified with and sought to be like him. I wanted to keep the safety of his presence with me by being like him, even when he wasn't there.

Even though I didn't see him much, I always felt Dad was there to protect me, and that he'd do whatever it took. Dad loved me, and I knew it.

There's one story about us driving home from Cape Cod, which is about four hours away from where we lived in New York City. When we were about halfway home, we realized we'd forgotten my favorite teddy bear and I started crying. So, without giving it another thought, Dad turned the car around to go get it, doubling the length of the trip. Thanks Dad! I love you too. *(By the way, I think I left another one in Portland, Oregon when I moved to Florida last winter. Any chance you can go get it for me now Poppa?)*

As an adult, I sometimes still draw on the "go back for the teddy bear" memory when I feel irrationally frightened. What memories might you treasure to see you through anxiety without binging?

Other Family Influences During My Earliest Years

During my preschool years I was mostly just with Mom, Dad, and my mother's parents *(Ma Pearl and Pa Mike)*. My father was more or less estranged from his family, so they almost never visited. His mother (Ma Esther) came once or twice. The only thing I remember about her was that when she babysat, she'd gave me a bath in the sink instead of the tub. I thought that was odd because to that point I'd only ever seen dishes washed there. But she convinced me, and I remember it was a lot of fun!

I tried taking a sink bath as a teenager when I remembered the event but I'm sure you know how that turned out.

CHAPTER 3: THE ELEMENTARY YEARS (5 TO 9)

All things considered, and notwithstanding the fact you'll clearly see how my food addiction was set up during this time, my elementary school years were utter bliss. My parents had just accomplished their first upwardly-mobile move to Great Neck, NY, a very well-to-do town on Long Island with schools ranked #12 in the entire nation. Granted, they bought one of the least expensive houses in the neighborhood to make this happen, but they were doing well and were extremely excited about it.

Move in day was April 18th,1969, which, oddly, is the same day I defended my dissertation 22 years later. My Dad had successfully exited the army without having to serve in Viet Nam, and I think both Mom and Dad were very relieved.

So there they were, two kids from troubled homes who'd fallen in love in junior high school, gotten married in college, created a family of their own, with one professional career in the saddle, and a nice house in a great neighborhood. They'd also made friends in the area and my dad was going to open a private practice. Dad's job at the hospital was paying him a decent wage, and we could afford to do fun family things each week like going to baseball (the Mets) and basketball (the Nets) games.

We were surrounded by good things and my parents felt hopeful on all counts. They'd created a stable, loving environment for my sister and I, which they'd never known themselves, and for that I'll be forever grateful. That said, my early food training clearly left something to be desired, and because the purpose of this book is largely to help you understand my journey out of food addiction, I'm going to focus on food-related memories and food-relevant lessons learned. The good, the bad, and the ugly.

My Very Hearty Daily Breakfast

In elementary school I'd wake up WAY earlier than everyone else in the household so I could go downstairs and watch cartoons by myself. Sometimes it was so early (e.g. 4:30 am) I had to watch agriculture shows first. Ever since, I've been an early riser. To this day I find early morning is my most productive time of day.

I rather enjoyed my time alone in the morning, but what really clinched the deal was Mom ensuring there'd always be a fresh, whole box of frosted chocolate fudge Pop-Tarts waiting for me. Every single goddamn day. I still remember the routine as if it were yesterday...

I'd take the Pop-Tart box out of the closet, place it neatly on its alter *(the table),* sit down and worship it for a second, then open the packages one by one. There were two in each, but I never understood why they didn't just have all six waiting for you when you opened the box. Were there really people who only ate one or two at a time? What a stupid waste of packaging material.

Anyway, after dispensing with the wrappers, I'd lay all six out on the table in a nice, neat little rectangle. Then, I'd nibble around the edges of each one, taking care not to touch the frosting or the filling. See, the edges tasted boring, and you didn't want to risk letting them ruin the experience of the good parts in your mouth. God forbid! Plus, having six edge-free chocolate Pop-Tarts staring you in the face, all alone at your kitchen table at 5:30 am was better than any experience I could imagine.

Once I'd safely disposed of the edges in my stomach, I'd see how slowly I could eat the good parts while watching my cartoons. I was in heaven.

Occasionally Mom would come down around 7 am and make scrambled eggs for me too, but I wasn't too interested. On the weekends she'd sometimes serve bagels and lox. But mostly, I started my days with a WHOLE BOX of Pop-Tarts. Like clock-work.

Although my breakfast experience messed up any chance of me even remotely understanding what healthy eating might look like as a child, to this day I think of these memories with nothing but fondness.

That said, I haven't eaten chocolate or refined sugar in years. My body can't handle it anymore. A five-year-old's pancreas is MUCH better able to manage the flood of sugar in the blood stream, and my liver can't process all the theobromine, caffeine, phenylethylamine (PEA), and anandamide in the chocolate anywhere near the way it did a half century ago. If I ate that breakfast today, I'd get so sick I'd have to sleep it off for at least a day. I'd also blow up like a balloon. Ever since I turned thirty a quarter century ago, I gain weight VERY quickly on sugar and flour.

I also know from my adult experience that chocolate kicks off a cascade of urges for me that are very difficult to manage. Virtually all my later binges started with chocolate, followed by something like a half dozen bagels, a box of muffins, one or two whole pizzas, etc.

Chocolate may be a fine and lovely thing for many people, but I'm decidedly not one of them. *I therefore chose to just live with the memories instead of the actual food party.* **Read that last sen-**

tence again please and ask yourself "What memories should I subtract food from and just enjoy for their own sake?"

You CAN thoroughly enjoy memories forever. There's nothing wrong with treasuring those feelings. In fact, by allowing yourself to do so it becomes more likely you'll be able to find a decent substitute. There's a difference between enjoying the memories and eating the associated junk. Don't throw out the baby with the bathwater.

My Brilliant Cafeteria Trades

In 1969 I went to Lakeville Elementary School, about one block from our home in Great Neck, NY. I used to walk there myself at five years old. It was only a block away, but as an adult I realize it was very risky for my parents to let me do that. I mean, I lived in a safe neighborhood and all, but still, how safe can a five-year-old ever be by himself?

Despite the risk, nothing traumatic ever came of it and I very much enjoyed walking. I still do.

Anyway, in the school cafeteria in 1st grade, I had what was perhaps my first food epiphany. See, Mom would always send me to school with a sandwich and a regular milk neatly packed in my Underdog lunch box. *(Underdog could totally take Superman, Spiderman, and the Hulk at the same time, with one hand tied behind his back! Don't think so? Bring it on!)* Mostly the sandwiches were peanut butter and jelly, but sometimes Mom gave me turkey, cheese, etc.

I didn't like sandwiches so much, but I figured out one of my six-year-old little buddies really did. As luck would have it, *his* Mom gave him chocolate milk every day, not regular milk. My first business deal in the making! Every day we'd trade half my sandwich for his entire chocolate milk. Then I found a girl whose mom also sent chocolate milk, so I traded her for the other half.

Therefore, most days I had TWO chocolate milks and one regular milk for lunch… and nothing else.

On rare occasion I could find a third kid who preferred regular milk to chocolate milk, and we'd swap too, so I could have me a big hairy THREE chocolate milk lunch! Considering I'd also eaten six chocolate fudge frosted Pop-Tarts for breakfast, and that we also had a daily milk-and-Oreo-cookies afternoon break in school, I think you might begin to get a sense of my childhood diet.

After School Eating

After school I'd walk home, grab an entire box of Sugar Pops, a few cans of Coca Cola, and go plop myself down in one of our ratty yellow bean-bag chairs in front of the TV. Sometimes my sister and I would play a board game or something. After that I'd play baseball with a friend before dinner, or incessantly ride my bike around the neighborhood. Thank goodness I was always an active kid!

I never did homework. I always finished it in school during the breaks because I didn't want anything to interrupt my after-school food orgy.

There were two brief hiatuses from the routine however, each for a few months.

In the 1st grade I fell in love with Denise Solomon and wanted to spend every waking moment with her. We would play house and talk about the kids we were going to have, and all the things we were going to feed them. Denise was stunningly beautiful with a smile that just wouldn't quit. But shortly after I asked her to marry me at six years old, her parents got wind of the situation. They had a meeting with my parents and decided we were too young to be in love, so they broke us up and we stopped playing together. I was devastated ☹

I also fell in love with a girl named Jill in the second grade and used to go to her house to play all the time too. I knew better than to get engaged the second time around, and we just drifted apart. Might've been our parents' schedules, who knows.

I suppose these stories are funny in retrospect, but they also make me sad, because they're illustrative of how my parents treated my later girlfriends. I don't recall them ever saying anything nice about anyone I dated in my youth, and this was, at least in part, responsible for me rebelliously running off and making the impulsive decision to get married at 22 years old, WAY before I was ready. *(It now does my heart good to see my sister so supportive of her daughter's relationship with her first boyfriend.)*

We can NOT blame our parents if we want to recover from food addiction. We must accept that we made our own life and food choices at every juncture, and we could've chosen to do otherwise. I wholeheartedly embrace that philosophy.

Still, I sometimes feel if I'd had a little more support in those early years I might have chosen better. But my parents were going through their own traumas, and they did much better with us than their parents did with them. There's really no comparison and I'm grateful.

After School Play Time

My grandpa Mike *(http://www.neverbingeagain.com/images/ PaMike.jpg)* was extraordinarily involved with me in my elementary years. He taught me all sorts of things. For example:

> **How to build a fire.** We'd do it every day and roast hot dogs in the blaze to gobble down thereafter.

> **How to play baseball.** He'd throw the ball with me whenever I asked. We'd make up pretend games. Sometimes the kids on the street would join in. He was stellar with chil-

dren.

➤ **How to exercise.** This one was very helpful. I used to hate running, so he said "Let's walk 90 steps for every 10 we run." Then, of course, it became 80/20, 70/30, etc., and before you knew it, I was running all the way around the neighborhood.

➤ **How to ride a bike.** Pa Mike got me onto my first tricycle. Then he both put on and took off the training wheels on my bike when it was time. Pa Mike always encouraged me to push past my fears. I still remember the day when I was only five years old that I first rode the two-wheeler. "Pa Mike, Pa Mike! I did it! I did it!" It's one of my fondest "yes I can" memories. Later, I'd draw upon this memory when I had an intense craving in order to reassure myself I could indeed keep my Pig in its Cage. *Pause here for a moment to search for one of your earliest "yes I can" moments. Write it down and ask yourself when you want to remember it?*

➤ **Electronic circuitry.** When I was 9 my grandfather taught me about electronic circuitry. Then he showed me how to connect a magnetic switch to a tape recorder and integrate it into a circuit. We wired that tape recorder up to the toilet seat so that whenever anyone opened the lid to sit down it would wait ten seconds and say "Oh no!!! Don't do it! There's somebody down here!" That went over really well with my parents, as you can imagine.

➤ **How to cook spaghetti, grilled cheese sandwiches, and cheeseburgers.** And that's all I knew how to cook until I was much older! None of these things are in my diet anymore. I still don't love to cook. I live mostly on smoothies and big salads. But I have learned a few delicious dishes, like spiralized cucumber noodles topped with raw tomato-lemon-date sauce with basil for example, which is every bit as satisfying as my spaghetti used to be.

➢ **How to play poker.** My sister and I used to sit with Pa Mike and Ma Pearl for hours on end playing poker and eating junk food. Of course, grandma and grandpa smoked like chimneys, so despite these fond memories there's a good chance I may die of lung cancer due to all the secondhand smoke... but I suppose nobody knew about that in the late 60s and early 70s. Still, I always hated the smell of cigarette smoke, and did everything I could to get my grandparents to stop, including threatening to pee on the tips when they weren't looking. *(Hey, don't judge - I was a very creative boy!)*

Before I was born my parents smoked too. We found this old picture very recently which really surprised me, since I'd never known either of them when they lit up. (http://www.neverbingeagain.com/images/DadSmoked.JPG)

Laurie told me she found evidence my mother never quit, but simply hid the lighters and cigarette packs around the house. She even once showed it to me deep in my Mom's closet, but my denial was too strong. I couldn't believe it. I now know my sister doesn't lie however, so I'd be shocked if it weren't true. I just hate thinking of Mom like that. I also know Mom always snuck junk food and said "don't tell Dad." It all makes sense. **If you've ever engaged in sneak eating, where might you have learned the habit?**

Due to work, Pa Mike spent a lot more time with me than my dad could, and as much as I loved my dad, Pa Mike was the primary male figure in my life during these years. Despite his criminal past, during the entirety of my life from birth to the day he died of a brain tumor in 1990, Pa Mike was an upstanding citizen...and a loving, nurturing grandfather.

I never knew about his history until I was an adult. Mom kept from me the fact he'd been in jail the entire time she was pregnant. I think she wanted me to see him for who he was, not who he'd been. I really respect her for this – it was the right thing to do.

I believe this experience is a good part of the reason I so strongly believe in redemption, even though I'm not a religious person. I think people deserve a second chance. I think, like Sartre' said, we can remake ourselves at any moment.

I've learned this is a critical perspective for recovering from binge eating. You CAN forgive yourself and become a different person. In fact, if you want to get better, you MUST. Anyone who decides to dedicate themselves to becoming a healthier person deserves every chance to be that person, no matter how long they've been binging, and no matter what they've done in their past.

Whatever it is you've done, whatever it is you feel guilty about, you're much more likely to figure out how you can make up for it if you forgive yourself and live out the balance of your life in a healthy way.

My grandpa made some very serious mistakes. But he made up for it to the best of his ability by pouring his love into me. Mom was always concerned about my closeness with Pa Mike. I think she thought he'd turn me into a criminal…

But between her fear, my grandfather's genuine desire to do good with me, and my father's dedication to be a great psychologist in the world…my experience with Pa Mike had the EXACT OPPOSITE impact. I became a real goodie-goodie who wanted to help. I get more gratification from helping people than making money. I get more gratification from helping people than just about anything else. I must FORCE myself to charge reasonable rates, not to pay employees too much, etc. I'm *overly* concerned about complying with the law and put myself at a competitive disadvantage relative to my peers. And I often take the short end of the stick in business deals to avoid taking advantage of people in any way. (*I compensate for this now by having a real shark for a business partner and letting him do the negotiating.)*

Pa Mike did good by me. I miss him terribly.

Who in your upbringing was misunderstood by your family? What positive impact did they have on you? How can you honor that more in your life today?

Dinner

Dinner was always something more substantial. We rotated a few favorites:

> **Tuna Casserole:** Macaroni, gobs of American cheese, cream of mushroom soup, tuna fish, served very warm. I could eat tubs of this!

> **Beef Stroganoff:** Rice, cream of mushroom soup, onion powder, and ground beef. I liked it, but it didn't hold a candle to Mom's Tuna Casserole.

> **Meatloaf:** Meat, eggs, ketchup, spices, rice.

> **Spaghetti and Meatballs:** "Consume mass quantities!"

> **Pizza:** "Consume mass quantities!"

> **Lamb Chops:** This was never of interest to me. Too fatty.

Desert was usually ice cream. Big tubs of ice cream. Mostly chocolate for me. But also pistachio-mint-chip, which was what my mother ate every day while I was in the womb.

Looking back at what was for dinner in my youth, it's no wonder I have always had an affinity for salty-starchy-fatty combinations. What was for dinner in your house when you were young?

Food at Home in General

Throughout my childhood my parents ensured food was always plentiful. I never went hungry. There was always something in the refrigerator to grab, or something on the table to eat. See, my parents had a home office in addition to their office in Manhattan, so there was ALWAYS food available for the patients.

The patients would come talk to my sister and I while they waited for their sessions. Big spreads of bagels and lox with cream cheese. Donuts. Chocolate. Rugalach. Chicken. Chopped liver. Cheese. Muffins. And during the holiday season Gefilte Fish, Matzoh, etc. I associated all this food with some of the most interesting and meaningful talks of my childhood. Unfortunately, while the talks were psychologically enriching in so very many ways, there wasn't much that was healthy about the food.

Every Saturday Ma Pearl and Pa Mike would come over with a big box of jelly donuts, rugalach, and (sometimes) black and white cookies from the bakery. Between all the morning cartoons and all the sugar, Saturday quickly became our favorite day of the week.

The "Eat It" Game

When I was about 9 my sister and I created our own board game called "Eat It." We literally took cardboard and drew out the game, created "eat it" cards you had to pick when you landed on an "eat it" square, and would sit and play the game with dice for hours at a time.

The "eat it" squares were the main point. Before we started, Laurie and I would each create several disgusting concoctions. Combinations of food you'd never eat together: A slice of pizza with grape jelly all over it. Fish with powdered sugar. Chocolate cake with mounds of salt. Or some type of a food volume challenge like "drink a whole gallon of water in under 10 minutes" or eat TWO boxes of chocolate fudge Pop-Tarts in the same time period. You get the idea. *(LEGAL: Don't try any of these challenges yourself please. The bad combinations are harmless enough, but you can actually die from drinking too much water all at once, etc.)*

Then each player would roll the dice in turn and go that number of squares. If you wound up on an "eat it" square you had to pick a card and take a few bites of whatever concoction was on it, or else go backwards twice the number of squares that got you there.

I eventually went way too far and started making concoctions like broccoli and boogers, salad with dirt, etc., so Laurie stopped wanting to play the game.

I never said I was normal with food, did I?

Our Food Fighting Babysitter

My sister and I often marvel at the parade of crazy babysitters who took care of us. One woman would eat all the food in the refrigerator after we went to sleep. Another told us we'd sold our souls to the devil, a memory which would haunt us for a decade.

Then there was Butch.

Before I tell you about Butch, let me just say up front I'm NOT proud of this story. As an adult I feel AWFUL about what it must've been like for my parents. I wish it never happened, but it did, and the reason I include it is because it contributed to my early confusion about what food was for, and my willingness to disregard the consequences about what you did with it.

So here goes...

Butch was the 19-year-old brother of my parents' friend Mary. He babysat for us one-and-only-one time when I was about eight years old, and Laurie was six. Butch showed up on a motorcycle, with his jaw wired shut from a recent accident. And soon after my parents went out with their friend, he made us a GIANT pot of spaghetti and meatballs.

It was really good, and I got full pretty fast. So I took the spaghetti remaining on my pate and placed it on my sister's plate instead. "Spaghetti on Laurie's plate" I distinctly remember saying.

Laurie did NOT love this idea, so she reciprocated in kind. "NO! Spaghetti on Glenn's plate!" she said.

This went back and forth a few times and we were all laughing about it, including Butch. But then, as I was prone to do in 1972, I took things to the next level. Grabbing mounds of spaghetti with my hands all at once, I threw it all on my sister's head. "Spaghetti on Laurie's HEAD!" I said with a smile...

Of course, Laurie returned the favor.

I think we each gave each other the spaghetti shampoo treatment twice before Butch decided to intervene, but NOT in the way you might think...

He yelled "Spaghetti on the CEILING!" as he grabbed two massive handfuls of pasta and launched it to the white stucco wall above us. We watched with complete fascination while most of it at first stuck, then slowly fell, noodle by noodle, leaving a big red spot behind.

Chaos ensued...

"Spaghetti on the WALLS!"

"Spaghetti on the FLOOR!"

"Spaghetti IN the CLOSET!"

"Spaghetti on the DOG!"

"Spaghetti on the COUCH!"

Etc., etc., etc.

Eventually, we ran out of spaghetti. Butch then made us go to our rooms while he feigned a half-hearted attempt to clean up...

Then, he came to my room with a big bottle of ketchup and said "Here, Glenn, put out your hands", into which he poured a massive wad of ketchup. "Now go put this on your sister's face."

I obliged, then went back to my room to lay down. Everyone knows a boy needs his rest after smushing his sister's face with a half bottle of ketchup, right?

About 2 minutes later my sister came running into my room, two hands filled with mustard, which she forced into MY face and onto my hair, also at the behest of our very respectable and responsible babysitter.

Then came a variety of other condiments, creams, and potions, before we eventually took showers and went to bed. If memory serves me correctly, mayonnaise was the worst one I experienced on my own face.

I can only imagine how my parents felt when they came home. We never got in trouble for it, nor even spoken to about it! I guess they held Butch responsible and just cleaned up. Or maybe they'd gotten very stoned with their friends, so when they came home, they just had a big ol' adult food fight themselves. *(I'm not kidding – it's a real possibility given their lives in 1972.)*

We only have Dad to ask now, and he doesn't remember. Or else he's keeping a very closely guarded family secret. I guess we'll never know.

It's a funny story, but it had a bad impact on me. See, there's a good reason we have rituals and boundaries with food. It's easier to be present while you're eating if there's a defined place, time, and manner in which you eat. You can better enjoy your food and feel it nourishing you. It's also easier to know when you've had enough, and to learn to portion out the food you put on your plate to your approximate level of hunger...

But what I took away from this event, and others like it, was that those boundaries didn't really exist, or at least not as firmly as they should have. I learned there were NO boundaries with food, and it didn't matter how much you took or what you did with it. There were no consequences.

I still recall the experience fondly because it was an outrageously fun time as a nine-year-old boy... but my adult self now wishes it were different, and I know I suffered for decades, at least in part due to this environment.

We did eat dinner together at the table every night. There was a lot of tension about who got to talk, and when...and I always wanted to sit in my Dad's chair. I think this is why I developed a preference for eating most of my calories alone. To this day, although I eat much, MUCH healthier, I don't usually choose to eat many calories when I'm dining with others.

I don't have a big sneak eating problem anymore, in the sense that I'd be comfortable having anyone view what I am eating at any time... but I don't particularly enjoy eating with other people. I think of restaurants, for example, as being a lot more for company than for food. This works out fine as most of what's served in restaurants isn't particularly healthy—there always seems to be way too much added sugar, salt, oil, starch, etc. in the sauces—but it's definitely a preference shaped by my childhood dining experiences.

Last, if we ever should perchance dine together, you and I, please know you needn't worry about me pouring food on your head, or smushing ketchup on your face. That was a one-time thing.

What eating preferences did you learn at your dinner table growing up? How do they persist to this day? To what extent do they serve you, and how might you like to change them, if at all?

Grandma's Psycho Toe-Flicking Episode

Once in a while, my parents would ask my grandparents to take care of us while they were on vacation. Pa Mike worked during the day as a short-order chef, so mostly grandma Pearl was watching us. I remember one day when I was 9 and my sister was 7 as iconic of her relationship with us.

We'd started out the morning as usual with Pop-Tarts and sugary cereal. Then we went to my parents' room to play Monopoly on the floor. Ma Pearl repeatedly came into the room with two cans of Coca Cola while we played. Remember, my Mom ordered a case every week. "Here, drink more!" she'd say enthusiastically.

Then grandma would sit down in a chair right next to us, take off her shoes, and insist we flick her toe.

No, you didn't read that wrong. Ma Pearl wanted her toe flicked...

We were supposed to firmly and repeatedly bonk it with our thumbs while it was the other person's turn in the game, and while we kept drinking our sugary soda. She'd laugh and smile the whole time. We just kept on flicking, drinking, and playing.

Whenever we finished a can, Ma Pearl would say "just throw it on the floor, I'll go get you another." Of course, we obliged.

After a few hours the whole room was covered in soda cans, and something suddenly shifted in grandma's eyes. The next toe flick agitated her to no end and she started screaming: "There are soda cans ALL OVER the floor!!! You kids are disgusting! You are f-----g animals! This is gross, I can't believe you!! Go to your rooms now while I clean this up! AND STOP FLICKING MY GOD DAMN TOE!!!"

Now, you may wonder why in the world I told you this very bizarre story. What possible relevance could my grandmother's psycho toe flicking have to overcoming overeating?

Actually, quite a bit.

During this particular Ma Pearl episode, I was actively encouraged to pursue sugar in a manic frenzy, consequences be damned *(despite the incredible mess it made.)* I also learned to expect denigrating verbal punishment when it was over.

This sad pattern became something I did to MYSELF for decades with sugar.

There's good news though, because as an adult, when I finally figured out how to stop overeating, I had a powerful, visual image to draw upon that would immediately wake me up the moment I thought about reaching for anything sweet off my Food Plan...

"Don't flick her goddamn toe!" I'd say to myself, and the whole experience would come flooding back in an instant. I'd be able to stop the binge before it happened because the immediate thought was "You know exactly where toe-flicking (breaking your Food Plan) leads!"

Sometimes toxic memories serve us well. Take a few moments to think about your most difficult memories, either with or without food. Then, ask yourself what destructive pattern you may have acquired from it. Finally, see if you can crystalize that memory into a short, memorable statement about what you want to STOP doing. You can call upon that statement/ image during moments of temptation.

It works MUCH better than you can imagine!

Every New Year's Eve

Every New Year's Eve, from as far back as I can remember until I was about twelve years old, my sister and I would go stay with Ma Pearl and Pa Mike to watch the ball drop on TV. From the moment we got there until we left the next afternoon, we were fed a torrent of sugar, fat, starch, and salt. Rugalach, noodles and cheese, donuts, chocolate, pizza, PopTarts, soda, licorice, cheeseburgers, ...they worked us up into a manic, frenzied food high.

I remember I thought it was funny to weigh myself before and after. I was usually up at least five pounds when it was over.

I was always just a little chubby during those years, but I was also a very active kid, growing quickly, so the weight would come off and it never got too bad. Pa Mike taught me to love playing sports and exercising, and my Dad reinforced it. Thank goodness or I would've been obese for sure.

But in adulthood, in order to recover from overeating, New Year's Eve became another one of those happy memories for which I had to avoid throwing out the baby with the bathwater. My grandparents, particularly Pa Mike, were coming from a loving place...it's just that food was the primary way they knew how to show their love. This was very common among Jewish immigrant families in the NYC area.

I can still remember Ma Pearl and Pa Mike's smiling faces, how excited we all got when the ball dropped, all the toys they gave us, and how much they interacted with us while we played with them. I even have some audio tapes of our time together which I treasure.

But the manic food frenzy? Not so much. Bad learning – I can let that go.

I'll live with the memories, not the Slop!

CHAPTER 4: THE TRAUMATIC YEARS – 9 TO 14

The end of elementary school through the beginning of high school was a traumatic period, probably the worst in my life. When I quote D.W. Winnicott's "The nightmare we fear most is the one we've already been through", this is the personal nightmare I fear. Everything really came apart in my life during these years...

But I'm NOT going to spend ages telling you everything that happened. It's painful to write, and more painful to read. At the same time, I DO want you to see how much power there is in knowing what your WORST nightmare is. It gives you the ability to say "that's never going to happen again" when your inner food enemy starts predicting awful things in order to scare you into overeating. It also helps cut to the root of the issue, rather than allowing yourself to get stuck ruminating on *substitute* issues in your contemporary life.

It's only by knowing your worst fears that you can conquer them. As you read through this you might want to ask yourself what nightmare you are REALLY frightened of, and what you'd do in the extremely unlikely event it ever happened.

One last thing before we get into it: The end of MY personal nightmare coincided with my first involvement with my own therapist. When I was about 14 years old my dad sat me down and said "Glenn, if you want to work things out in life, get into therapy. If you REALLY want to work them out, become a therapist." I took that to heart and couldn't wait to see my own counselor.

It's a lot easier to face these things with the assistance of a licensed professional. So, if you're struggling, don't hesitate to find a good therapist. Remember to shop for them like you shop for anything else. Don't just judge by who takes your insurance. Call at least a half dozen and see how they respond. Most should spend some time with you on the phone first. If you ask them "How do you decide when to intervene with clients and when to just let them talk?" and "How do you know when therapy is done?" you will get a sense of whether the professional has an actual method to their madness, or just goes by the seat of their pants. I find those with an actual method tend to get better results.

OK, enough of that.

But I DO have one last-last thing before I tell you about this period...

Please know my personal traumas pale in comparison to stories I've heard from so very many patients over the years. For example, I once worked with a man who told me how his father beat and raped him virtually every day of his life. Women who were forced into prostitution. People who've lost their children to suicide. Those who were chained to their bed most of the day as children.

When you talk to as many people as intimately as I have *(I've seen probably 1,500+ clients at this point in my life)* you realize the world is, in many ways, a VERY cruel place. Civilization is a relatively recent experiment. So much of "humanity" is still, at its core, brutal. I wish it were otherwise, and I know my position is biased because the people I've seen are arguably those most troubled... but still, it's brutal out there.

In comparison to so much of what I've heard, I've really led a charmed life. And, my parents did the best they could. They had a MUCH rougher upbringing than they gave my sister and myself.

I DO still have hope for humanity because I've ALSO heard amazingly inspiring stories from truly wonderful people. Indeed, part of the reason I work so hard to do what I do is because I want to contribute to the upswing in wellbeing, morality, and compassion in the world. Despite what I've been through and everything I've seen, I've come out the other side feeling inspired and motivated to make a difference. I'm decidedly NOT nihilistic or pessimistic. I think civilization IS progressing. For example, it's now almost universally accepted around the globe that slavery is immoral. We couldn't have said that a few hundred years ago. We're growing. Slowly, but we are.

OK, so let's get into it.

When I was 9 years old, my parents decided to have an open marriage, having only been with each other since they were in junior high school. Although I think they did their very best to put the family first, the truth is, it was destabilizing. Suddenly there were weekends when either Mom or Dad wasn't around without any solid explanation. And you could feel a shift in each of them. The best way I could describe it is that you could sense great tension between them, combined with a kind of manic excitement they must have had about their new partners.

In some ways it was nice to have more special time with both Mom and Dad, as when the other was traveling the one at home would spend more focused time and energy with us. But really, it wasn't good. I went through several very bad things during that period, which I now understand to be my way of processing the insecurity and conflict I felt in the home at the time:

> ➢ **When I was 9, I briefly became anorexic.** My schoolteacher taught a class on how to count calories, and I got obsessed. I tried to minimize every last one. It was clearly an effort to gain some control in an environment which felt out of control. At one point, I got way too thin and passed

out on the floor in the supermarket from not eating. Mom revived me with a whole stack of chocolate bars. Thankfully, when she finally noticed I was becoming obsessed and took me to the doctor, it didn't take much to turn things around. I went right back to my old food-loving ways. Chocolate, sugar, pizza, pasta, cereal. This whole period only lasted a few months and I never returned to it again.

➤ **The same year I also came down with a serious case of pneumonia after my first summer at sleep-away camp.** I remember not being able to breathe. It was terrifying. I would get dizzy and fall when I tried to stand up and walk on my own. I was sure I was going to die. I obsessed about it all day long. Thankfully, I survived. But it was terrifying.

➤ **At ten years old, my parents sent me to Hebrew school, and I hated it.** I was a very big boy, already almost 6 feet, but I let the other kids pick on me. See, there was a lot of emphasis on valuing people's feelings in my household, but nobody taught me to stand up for myself. I think the bullies sensed the instability and insecurity I was feeling at home at the time too. An insecure big kid is the most delicious bully meat. So, I promptly stopped going to Hebrew School. I mean, I got into the carpool and got out at the front doorstep, cheerfully waving goodbye to my friend's mother when she dropped us off at the front door...but as soon as she left we'd all just head to the bagel store around the corner. Bagels were only 14 cents and I could buy a half dozen with the dollar Mom made sure I had with me each day. Hey! What was I supposed to do?

A few years later, in the 7th grade, I singled out the biggest bully in the school and punched him in the face when he started picking on my friend Robert. That knocked him right the hell down and put a complete end to the teasing and bullying...but it was humiliating while it lasted.

➤ **In the sixth grade, my parents decided to take us to Hawaii** *(Kauai)* **just before Thanksgiving break.** We were supposed to stay through the Thanksgiving and then return home, but my sister got pneumonia and was advised against flying because it was a long way back to New York. Dad was thrilled to be in the tropics and had just discovered credit cards... so we decided to stay through New Year's.

Then Mom got pneumonia, so, we wound up staying a few weeks longer. When I got home, Mom said "No real point going back to school now since it's almost time for the February break." So I didn't go to school from mid-November to mid-February.

When we finally got back to school, I was WAY behind on schoolwork, but that wasn't the real problem. I was always very smart and could catch up in my sleep. My intelligence is the one thing I've never questioned in my life – I've always had that confidence.

What was a real disaster was GIRLS. It seems from the time we left until the time we got back, the boys in the class had decided girls were no longer icky. Now it was cool to date and kiss them and stuff. But I never got the memo, and I felt like I'd landed in the twilight zone. Wait! Ewwwww! Gross!!!

I always remember one specific moment like it was yesterday. The prettiest girl in the class (Jill) pulled her chair up to me and said "look who I get to sit next to!" I froze like a deer in the headlights and sat there with a stupid look on my face and my mouth gaping open. I didn't say a word. Jill promptly pulled her chair back, and thereafter NONE of the girls flirted with me. It was pretty awful, and I didn't know what to do about it, so I just withdrew.

From that day forward I had the hardest time asking girls out. And we didn't have social media or dating sites back then so mostly I didn't date in high school. Looking back on things, I think, sadly, junk food became my girlfriend.

➢ **At 11 years old, I developed Osgood-Schlatter's disease.** Basically, bad knees due to growing too fast, but I exaggerated it in my head and became convinced I couldn't walk. I think I just needed the attention, and I walked on crutches for a full year. I made a few good friends in junior high who helped me carry my books and such between classes, but it really wasn't worth the sacrifice. I grew out of it in one year, but not before going all the way through summer camp without running or playing sports. Physically, I felt I wasn't like the other kids. I couldn't compete.

➢ **At 12 years old, we had a big conflict with my grandmother that caused her and my grandfather to walk out of our lives for four entire years.** I still remember the day. It was the night before my parents' vacation and my grandparents were going to look after us while Mom and Dad were gone. Ma Pearl was insisting I have my friends come visit ME instead of letting me go to their houses as usual... because she'd be too worried if I wasn't home after school.

I was understandably upset since I'd developed some very good friends, and we'd had regular after school routines which required I go to their houses as frequently as they came to mine. I'd be utterly humiliated to tell them "grandma won't let me." I voiced this concern, and it escalated into a big family conflict. We ALL said awful things about my grandmother. She was indeed a kook and a half —*much worse than a worry wart (recall the Psycho Toe Flicking story)*—but she definitely loved and nurtured us too and didn't deserve to be ambushed like that by any stretch of the imagination.

She and my grandfather got up and left. I was thereafter encouraged to think of them as "bad" or "crazy" people, mostly by Mom, though Dad didn't seem to mind since I think he was thrilled to have Mom to himself in the house again. I didn't see or talk to Ma Pearl or Pa Mike again for four years. Even after they were back in our lives, things were never the same.

I lost them. It was awful. Particularly losing my grandfather. I remember going to visit him on his death bed about 12 years later and feeling devastated. What had I done? I was only a child, but it was a very, very hard lesson to learn.

Unfortunately, I didn't see the connection and repeated the estrangement with my own parents for many years. I wish I had a time machine so I could do it all over again. It's my biggest regret in life.

➢ **When I was thirteen, the night before Valentine's Day, I had a mini breakdown of sorts**. I wasn't quite delusional, but I wasn't quite sane either. I'd been studying my dad's hypnosis books and I was convinced I could hypnotize the other kids in school without them knowing it. I stayed up all night writing a crazy letter to Jill *(the pretty girl who'd pulled her chair up to me when I was 10)* explaining this super-power I'd developed.

I showed Mom the letter and she encouraged me to call Jill and read it to her. Not the best dating advice I ever got. Jill was very nice about it, but I clearly overwhelmed her, and she didn't want much to do with me thereafter. Rightfully so. She always said hello with a nice smile in the hallway though – that meant a lot to me.

One more thing – toward the end of this period my Mom started making a lot of very fatty food. Spicy, fatty lamb. Tons of cheese-laden dishes. A lot of fatty deli meat. Salami, pastrami, corned beef. Fatty food has never digested well in my system, and I genuinely believe it was partly responsible for overwhelming my psyche.

I've since learned it's particularly bad to eat a high carbo-hydrate diet when it's also laden with fat, because the fat serves as an insulator in the blood and makes it hard for the sugar to leave the bloodstream. This apparently con-tributes to atherosclerosis and other sugar-metabolic dis-orders... while simultaneously sapping your physical and mental energy. When we get to the part of the book which details which specific dietary philosophies were most help-ful to me, you'll see that, at least for me, a big leap out of binge eating had to do with seriously limiting these fats.

I think the end of my traumatic period came about when my parents realized the open marriage wasn't working for either them or their children. I specifically remember Dad sitting me down when I was about to have my first date—*which he set up for me with a friend's daughter*—and telling me monogamous ro-mance was the most important thing in the world. He told me to treasure a woman, and only one woman, like she was all that mattered. He said to be sure she knew how I felt about her. He helped me buy a book of poems to share with my date.

I'm pretty sure Dad wanted me to do better than he did. I think this talk was his way of making good. I internalized this senti-ment on the deepest level, and have never lost the yearning for monogamous, romantic love. I think it was seriously misplaced in my marriage, at least during the second half. *(The first five to ten years were nice).*

My Mom also took me to see her therapist (Betsy) right as this period was coming to an end, and it was extraordinar-ily helpful to me. I realized that putting your experiences into words and sharing them with another human being had an in-credibly transformative impact if that other human handled it correctly. This principle became a big part of my thinking and found its way into the Never Binge Again philosophy.

Words are the food of the intellect. When we can put our previously traumatizing thoughts into words, our adult intellect can organize the experience in a much more rational, logical manner. The fear is thus dramatically neutralized, and we are free to make other, more rational behavioral choices.

Never Binge Again focuses on disempowering the logical fallacies and lies the Reptilian part of our brain fosters regarding the junk we crave. It specifically says it's unnecessary to use this process to solve your emotional difficulties before you stop overeating. In fact, the opposite is true – you're more likely to solve your emotional difficulties if you use Never Binge Again to stop overeating first!

Notwithstanding this position, you should know the evolution of the methodology for disempowering the Reptilian Brain did come straight out of my early experiences with psychotherapists. And you CAN utilize it to take control of your emotional reactions and traumas too. Just don't make the mistake of thinking it's necessary to do so in order to stop binging!

The last thing I'll say here is that most often when people revisit the traumas and tragedies from their childhood, there is the danger that their Reptilian Brain will use it to suggest they are "damaged" and incapable of overcoming overeating. But the truth is, adversity doesn't only do damage. Adversity can forge character strengths too.

> Being anorexic for a few months at 9 years old is an experience I never want to have again. That memory acts like a kind of trampoline to bounce me back into normal territory whenever I start to become too restrictive. That's a character strength which has served me for a lifetime.

> Being seriously ill with pneumonia as a child caused me to face my fear of death at an early age. Having stared death in the face—*even just in my imagination*—gave me much more appreciation for life. It gave me strength to treasure the present moment. It's part of how I developed the binge-

busting mantra "I always use the present moment to be healthy!"

➤ Having been bullied and *(eventually)* knocking the bully down gave me the confidence to know I could deal with other bullies too. My Pig for example.

➤ Being unable to walk for a while as a child *(at least in my own mind)* taught me how to ask others for help when I needed it.

➤ Walking to the edge of sanity and (almost) developing a delusion showed me how my mind is structured, and what it was capable of under extreme stress. Since that point I've learned to recognize when I'm getting carried away with any given idea. I think it's made me a much MORE grounded and realistic person. In fact, I believe my core strength as a therapist emanates from my ability to face reality and help others to do the same. People rely on me to check their own perception of events, and to tell them in a gentle way how the world really is.

Adversity forges character, and character helps you to dominate the Lizard Brain. Being able to stop myself from getting carried away with irrational fantasies made it more possible to catch the Pig when it told me "one bite won't hurt" or "you can get away with it" or "just start tomorrow", etc.

You might wish to pause here and ask yourself if there's a traumatic memory you'd like to put in writing. After writing the details in full, ask yourself what you learned. How did it forge a piece of your character? What strength will you carry forward because of it?

It's very gratifying to do this. But like I said, if it's too upsetting, please do it with the assistance of a licensed professional.

In any case, there WERE some very interesting stories from this time period which had very nice thematic lessons built in. I'll leave you with two, beginning with a strange encounter my Mother, sister, and I had with two pimps in Manhattan.

Pimps Is Good People Too? A Life Lesson from 1975

https://www.neverbingeagain.com/images/
GlennTheGreat.jpg

I was eleven years old in 1975. I'd lived a very sheltered life in Great Neck, NY, but that all changed that summer. And no, I'm not talking about puberty. That was relatively uneventful, with the possible exception of an incident I won't go into with a girl nick-named "Big Kim" ...but I digress.

I'm talking about one very frightening drive home from Manhattan to Great Neck with my sister and my Mom. Mom was seeing clients in midtown as a fledgling psychotherapist. I forget exactly why Laurie and I were with her that day, but I'll NEVER forget the ride home.

Driving across mid-town Manhattan during a hot summer day's rush hour is about as thrilling as watching an earthworm cross the street, just a lot slower. The traffic was brutal, so Mom chose to take a detour through Harlem. It was easier to go straight uptown and head east on 125th street than to try and get anywhere on 57th *(around the corner from Mom's office.)* So uptown we went.

Harlem was quite a site for a spoiled Great Neck kid. Remember, this was 1975, and Harlem was a far cry from what it is today, thanks to the previous mayor's anti-crime efforts. As a boy, I'd heard all the stories on TV, the shootings, stabbings, drug dealers, prostitutes, muggers, etc. I'd expected to see a veritable prison ward loose on the streets, but what greeted us instead was a friendly, busy neighborhood with street vendors and men dressed in all sorts of ways. Some wore suits and ties, others donned jeans and a t-shirt, and still others were adorned in a ridiculous amount of "bling", though we didn't have that word back then.

We even passed a street juggler and a guitar player.

The whole scene lit up my eyes with wonder! That is, until Mom turned down a side street and the car stalled. She seemed a little worried, so of course my sister and I were too. But Mom remained calm and said we should just sit there for a moment.

So we did. And then it happened...

A large, pink Cadillac with fuzzy dice pulled up behind us, and two large, lean black men got out and started walking toward our car. Mom turned to Laurie and I in the back seat and said "You guys have been great kids and I love you very much. But we're probably going to die now, and I want you to know it's OK."

For all you parents looking for someone to emulate, let me just say here and now, that was NOT the best mothering tactic in the world. A giant wave of anxiety shot through me. I'd like to say I was planning some macho, heroic maneuver...but let's face it, I was eleven and didn't even shave yet. I'm lucky I didn't poop my pants.

Before I knew it, the men were on both sides of the car, motioning for Mom to roll down the window. She did. I'm not sure she had any other choice. Then, much to our surprise, the men didn't take out any guns or knives. Instead, they gently leaned into the car and said to her "Is everything alright, Sistah? Your kids OK?"

Mom just smiled and said yes.

"What's the matter then Sistah, car won't start?"

The rest of the conversation I don't remember.

What I DO remember is that shortly thereafter the two nice men began pushing the car over a half mile to the garage they were most familiar with, my Mom, Laurie, and myself inside. Then they drove us all the way home in their big pink Cadillac 35 miles to Great Neck!

As we said goodbye, mom offered them $50 for their troubles— *a lot of money back then*—but they refused saying "We're all family on the road, Sistah!"

Now, you might think these guys would've shown up later expecting my mother to, um, "work for" them, but they simply took off and we never heard from them again. That was my first exposure to Harlem. The people we THOUGHT were our worst enemies in a terrifying situation were the ones who saved us!

This experience opened me up a LOT to a wide variety of different types of people. It was extraordinarily helpful to me not only in the rest of my adolescence, where I found myself equally as comfortable with the straight A students as I did with the punk rockers and stoners, but especially as a psychologist later on. I guess, in the end, it taught me never to judge a book by its cover...

For example, when I was a hospital intern just before getting my doctorate, I recall doing an intake interview with a 400-pound Hell's Angel. He had scars all over his head, donned a shiny leather jacket, and rode into the parking lot on a very loud Harley Davidson motorcycle. I politely greeted him in the lot, walked him back to my office, closed the door, and sat down behind my desk. The first thing he said was "So, college boy, I'm here because I beat up 8 police offers with my head last night, and they said I had to come see you. Tell you the truth, I'd like to run through YOU with my head right now, college boy!"

I can't say I handled it perfectly, but because of my experience in 1975 I wasn't anywhere near as frightened as most people would've been. That lack of fear made it possible for me to hold my ground and talk to the guy like a normal person. Turns out once I did, he was a real Teddy Bear. I was very sad the hospital wouldn't let me work with him further. I think he was too. *(The intern doing the intake wasn't always assigned the patient – I'm sure my superiors had their reasons, but I never understood this practice.)*

I could tell you dozens of similar stories. There's ALWAYS a reason for the exterior image people present. A story behind the story. After decades of experiencing this time after time I developed a little mantra to remind myself of this...

When I encounter any level of what I perceive to be unnecessary aggression, anxiety, or upset in another person I ask myself "How does everyone else react to this person?" Then I say to myself "**Be Kind**", which reminds me to think about what this person genuinely needs before I react in the same way everyone else must.

Don't react to aggression with aggression. Don't react to anxiety with anxiety. Don't react to impulsiveness with impulsiveness. Be quiet. Think for a minute. Be present. Ask another question. Make a neutral comment. ANYTHING but what I imagine is the reflexive reaction the person in front of me must engender in people all the time.

When I can do it— *(it's a muscle that needs to be developed and maintained)*—I'm amazed at the results. If I can patiently get through a few difficult moments, people share the most meaningful things. I often remember these experiences as the defining moments in the relationship, and some of the most powerful interactions of my career.

The therapeutic word for this is "Corrective Emotional Experience." I'm giving the person a human interaction they aren't used to. See, most people who walk around aggressing on others wind up experiencing the whole world as an aggressive place. Their aggression seems justified because people either aggress back on them or run away screaming. They don't experience love. They don't experience kindness. It's a self-fulfilling prophecy that snowballs downhill.

The same thing is true for very anxious people. Anxiety is contagious. People around an anxious person tend to respond to their anxiety with anxiety themselves. Or else they try to find closure for the surface level content of the person's anxiety too quickly by impulsively suggesting a solution. There is no deep investigation, which only makes the person more anxious that the listener can't possibly have a good solution. The result is that the anxious person never experiences a calm, loving interaction with others. They begin to believe that relationships only equate to progressively more anxious experiences. Another self-fulfilling, downward rolling snowball.

But if you can avoid reacting in the way everyone else reacts you can break the pattern. It's very gratifying, both for the person you're relating to but also for yourself.

I feel so strongly about this and have seen it work so well *(and so often)*, that I had the words "Be Kind" tattooed on my left arm. *(That tattoo was also inspired by a woman I was very much in love with at the time I got it. She did it to remind herself of her pledge to never harm another living being. Don't worry, I'm not covered in tattoos or anything – I don't want to ruin your image of me. Be Kind is one of only two on my body. The other is also a phrase. I'll tell you what it is later before this book is over.)*

I'm not saying I approve of pimping or prostitution in ANY way. To the contrary, I think the fact it still exists at such a broad level in our society is a scourge that requires a lot more attention, resources, and focus. What I AM saying is that behind every awful behavior there is always still a real person. If you can avoid rushing to judgment you might not only learn something but empower that person to come out and stop the bad actions. "Be Kind" can also make your daily interactions a lot less stressful, as people dare to trust you and drop their onerous, stress inducing behaviors around you.

Last, I don't know for certain those two men were pimps. They might've just been fans of Starsky and Hutch and decided to emulate them. Or maybe they just really, really liked pink Cadillacs and fuzzy dice. Who am I to judge?

Be Kind. Act differently than everyone else does in response to bad behavior. You'll be surprised what blessings this brings!

Summer Camp

During the years from 9 to 14, I went to sleepaway camp every summer. The first few weeks at the very first camp I was extraordinarily homesick. I remember my neighbor from across the street went with me, and we would meet in secret to have crying fits. "WE MISS OUR MOMMIES" we would say while we cried and cried and cried. It was pathetic. I was clearly not the most stable child! But at least we had the good sense to do this out of the vision of the other kids.

Thankfully, this only lasted a little while, but we both made heroic attempts to get our mothers to let us come home during this time. For example, every day I wrote a letter home saying I had poison ivy and the camp infirmary was refusing to treat it. I'd tell Mom how badly it itched. Then I'd add something about how awful the counselors were, that the activities sucked, and that I couldn't sleep because the kid in the bunk above me was always masturbating. *(The last part was the only part that was true).*

This came to an end when Chet, my extremely sensitive and skilled bunk counselor caught me alone one day. He told me that a lot of the other kids were very homesick and asked if I was homesick too. I burst out crying. Then he did something interesting...

He said he was sure the other kids looked up to me. I was the tallest kid in the group, and most physically mature. He asked me if I could help him make some of the other kids more comfortable at camp. He thought the best way to do that would be to create a baseball team and really encourage everyone. He wanted me to play first base.

I accepted, and the homesickness literally melted away instantaneously. I had SO much fun on first base. More importantly, it was my first lesson in leadership...

You get so much more from it than you give. Ever since that day I've wanted nothing but to help others.

Anyway, thereafter I only sent letters requesting massive amounts of candy and binge food. For example, this one here (http://www.neverbingeagain.com/images/
PleaseSendCandyMom.jpg). I was such a good little binge eater, wasn't I?

Running Away to the Basement

When I was about 10 years old my sister and I were very upset that my parents kept leaving us with crazy babysitters. We felt we were old enough to take care of ourselves and became very determined to prove it. So, we decided to run away from home... to the basement.

Mom saved the runaway letter I wrote her, and I digitized it to save for all eternity. You can see it here: http://
www.neverbingeagain.com/images/
WeRanAwayToTheBasement.jpg . I'll type it out for you in case you can't read the writing:

"Dear Mom:

We are proving to you that we are responsible enough to take care of ourselves. We have taken enough supplies to last us until tomorrow at 2:00 pm. We promise to be back at 2:00 pm tomorrow morning. This is very important to us. We promise that if we can't make it, we will come back.

We will go to the kitchen tomorrow at 2:00 pm exactly.

PS – Please don't look for us or get crazy about it. We will be fine. I have taken every precaution needed.

Your Kids,

Glenn Livingston and Laura Livingston"

Now, you might wonder what precautions I meant when I said "I've taken every precaution."

Basically, that meant I took a great big pot for us to pee and poop in, several boxes of Pop-Tarts, a blanket, and some pillows. Now, that wasn't AS crazy a plan as leaving us with Butch the baby-sitter (or Ma Pearl the toe flicker) … but we were back upstairs even before Mom had a chance to read the letter. Why? Because, well… let's just say peeing and pooping with your sister in a big pot in the basement isn't all it's cracked up to be.

What can we learn from this crazy story? A few things.

First, many of us will do crazy things in order to protect, preserve, and prove our autonomy. I really THOUGHT I knew how to take care of myself for a night. I didn't seek any outside guidance or assistance. I could've asked the librarian at school for books on what you needed to camp out. I could've talked to my uncle or my grandfather, who wouldn't have told my parents. I know that's not healthy, but they wouldn't have. I could have asked my friends if they'd ever stayed alone, how they fed themselves, etc. I could've even asked my sister for ideas…

But I didn't.

I was intent on proving I could do it all by myself, no matter what, no matter what, no matter what.

Which, coincidentally, is how I got myself in a lot of trouble with food over the years. Ultimately the solution for me came through an exhaustive amount of reading and consulting outside of the clinical psychology profession. I read nutritional books. I read various diet authors. I read about neurology. I read about addiction treatment.

Unfortunately, though, I didn't do this reading until after I'd wasted decades trying to solve the problem from a strictly psychological approach. My best thinking at the time was, if I could figure out and fill the hole in my heart, I wouldn't have to keep trying to fill it with chocolate, pizza, and muffins. In retrospect, this was just as wrongheaded as thinking I could pee and poop all night long into a bucket with my sister in the basement.

Being pigheaded and asserting your autonomy no matter what is a normal developmental stage. But I find many people never grow out of it, and there's usually some element of an autonomy conflict associated with binge eating. I find I have to thoroughly respect and support people's autonomy about their Food Plan, even or perhaps especially when I vehemently disagree, in order for them to eventually come around to something more reasonable.

Usually the pigheadedness involves a relentless desire NOT to accept that there's some food-like substance that needs either regulation or elimination in their diet. Sugar, flour, alcohol, and caffeine are the biggest culprits. Now, I'm NOT saying that everyone must give up or even regulate these things. What I AM saying is that if you're struggling, I might save you a few years of pain by suggesting you take a closer look at these "big four." Or even do a 30-day experiment without them entirely and see what you think thereafter.

You might be insisting on running away to the basement... and I promise you, it's better upstairs.

My First Experience in My Dad's Practice

When I was eleven, I started reading my Dad's psychotherapy books. I actually bugged his office when I was nine and listened to a bunch of sessions before Mom caught me, but we won't tell him that now OK? Just fair warning, if you ever see a therapist at their home and you know they have kids, you might want to bring some counter-espionage equipment.

That was in 1975, so I'm pretty sure the statute of limitations has expired. If not, oh well... I guess you can come visit me and my new husband "Bubba" living inside four grey walls. Please bring me some fresh fruit, leafy greens, and something to write with.

Anyway, I was particularly interested in the interpretation of dreams, and I told my dad about that interest. So, he suggested I come to one of his groups and talk about a dream. He'd show me how to work with it...

I did, and he did. And it was GREAT. I remember the dream *(something about a purple turtle)*, but I don't remember the interpretation we arrived at. Instead what I remember is the process he used to get there. He asked me about each element of the dream. All I had to do was tell him what it reminded me of, and I wasn't allowed to say "I don't know" ... I had to say what occurred to me, or what it MIGHT remind me of, and then the other people in the group would say what it might mean to them if THEY had had the same dream.

It was exhilarating. Whatever it was I talked about, I felt very relieved and excited afterwards. It filled me with energy. That was the moment I REALLY knew I wanted to become a psychologist, and I never wavered thereafter.

The mindset I learned in that group has direct impact on how to solve overeating problems. Many times people come to me asking why they can't stop eating...

Of course, the first thing I do is help them to reframe the question itself. Because if you ask yourself "why can't I stop overeating?" what you're really doing is programming your brain to find evidence that you can't stop. The more evidence your brain collects, the more you'll believe you really can't stop overeating, the more of a *failure* identity you'll develop. In contrast, if you ask "How can I stop overeating?" you'll be programming your brain to collect evidence that you CAN stop, and you'll develop a success identity.

But then, I ask them another question: "What's the single smallest thing you could and WOULD do, without any possibility of failure, that would make a big difference and set your ship moving in the right direction, or at least stop it from going further in the wrong one?"

To this question their Pig often grabs their tongue and says "I don't know."

But "I don't know" is not an acceptable answer if you want to stop overeating, because if you don't know then NOBODY does. The thing of it is, you DO know. Everyone knows. And to get there, you have to say what OCCURS to you. What MIGHT the answer be? You have to be willing to speculate, or else there's nothing that anyone else can help you with.

It's worth reading the last three paragraphs again, because "we don't know" is your Pig's second greatest weapon. *(The first is "we are powerless over these desires.")* If you're willing to take the "I don't know" weapon away from your Pig, there's virtually nothing you can't accomplish.

YOU MIGHT WANT TO STOP AND ANSWER THE QUESTION RIGHT NOW: "What's the single smallest thing you could and WOULD do, without any possibility of failure, that would make a big difference and set your ship moving in the right direction, or at least stop it from going further in the wrong one?"

CHAPTER 5: HIGH SCHOOL AND COLLEGE

In the 9th grade my parents started asking me to attend group marathons—therapy events held in a retreat center anywhere from several days to one full week. There was crying, screaming, talking, and hugging. Lots of hugging.

It was both a blessing and curse...

In the long run, exposure at such a young age to all the psychological ideas, learning how to empathize with how people think on the deepest level, and understanding how intimate relationships worked (*or didn't*) did wonders for my career. It also made me, modesty aside, an exceptionally sensitive and compassionate person.

On the other hand, I was constantly immersed with adults when I should've been spending time with people my own age. I became obsessed with this kind of contact. And, in contrast to the monogamous philosophy my father consciously tried to inculcate in me, I was flirting and cuddling with (*but not sleeping with or kissing*) a LOT of different women. Very attractive people twice my age.

It was very confusing, and I think contributed towards me having a lot of trouble dating in high school. I got a kind of inflated view of myself because all these wonderful women were surrounding and loving me. I came to expect women to adore me like my father's patients did, and when girls my age in the REAL world didn't naturally do that, I didn't understand and took it as rejection. This caused me to develop a severe shyness around girls my own age and was a big part of the reason I didn't really date in high school.

This didn't bother me too much, however, because I had Pop-Tarts, chocolate bars, pasta, tuna casserole, Cheez Wiz, Ritz Crackers, spaghetti and meatballs, pizza, meatloaf, and grilled cheese sandwiches to keep me company.

Seeing this pattern has been helpful to me in overcoming overeating, by the way, because I know there was a developmental phase that I missed—normal dating in high school—which caused me to retreat and not take certain types of risks. I was married when I really recovered from binge eating, so it wasn't appropriate that I resume taking those risks... but there were other types of interpersonal risks I COULD take. Making important business connections and asking to have lunch, for example.

Every time I took a risk despite my fear, I felt stronger and more secure inside. I noticed it was more comfortable to eat normally. Which is NOT to imply that it's necessary to be comfortable and/or feel secure in order to stop overeating—*you can stop despite any level of discomfort and insecurity!* —but why be uncomfortable if you don't have to be?

You might wish to pause and ask yourself if there are any normal developmental phases you missed because of your own overeating. Dating, friendship, learning how to earn money and feel independent, etc. If so, what steps could you take to improve these areas of life and resume learning, now that you've dedicated yourself to putting binge eating behind you?

In any case, the intense immersion in psychotherapeutic groups, combined with having my own once a week therapist made things a LOT better in high school. I also made a friend

(Richie) who's stayed with me throughout life. We've literally known each other for 40 years...

In high school, Richie and I smoked a lot of weed together, but we both grew out of that in college. In fact, in college I decided I simply didn't like the way either pot or alcohol affected my system. I discovered it left me depressed for several days afterwards. No judgment on people who like to have a little occasionally, but I realized it just was NOT for me, so I quit.

Cold Turkey...

I did NOT go to a program...

I didn't talk to a therapist about it...

I just outright quit...

And, other than one sip of champagne at my Ph.D. graduation dinner in 1991, I haven't had a drop or a toke for thirty-three years!

This has always been an important reference point in my life. I'd read so much about how alcohol and drugs were super addictive. You weren't supposed to be able to quit on your own if you got to a certain point with them... but I did. I just decided I wanted them out of my life, and boom, they were!

I would constantly think about this when I struggled with food in the future. It served as the success story which kept me going. I knew that if I could get drugs and alcohol out of my life simply as a matter of free will, there MUST be a way to do that with addictive food as well. I just was confused by all the misinformation out there that directed me to focus on my psychological wounds instead.

Pause for a moment here to ask yourself what you might use for your own success story? Was there ever something which "dogged" you... that you eventually managed to change? For some people it's quitting smoking. For others it was finally

learning a language. Or how to dance. Or juggle. Or do a headstand in yoga. Take the time to latch onto one or two key successes in your life and write them down so you can call upon them as needed.

Ignore your Pig's inevitable attempt to tell you there are none. If you're alive and reading this, you've had at least SOME success. I mean, at minimum, you learned how to read, right?

"Super Pig" is Born

Towards the tail end of high school, and mostly during the summer right afterwards, I discovered exercise, big time. I started running and bike riding again and lifting weights. Soon I realized that if I worked out hard for a few hours a day I could eat fricking EVERYTHING in whatever quantities I wanted to...

And therein, Super Pig was born.

I basically turned myself into a 6'4" eating, exercising, sleeping, and pooping machine. Workout, eat some Slop, sleep it off, poop it out, and then repeat.

In retrospect I realize I did NOT think this was a problem. I thought it was a superpower! *(Thanks to Doug Graham, author of "The 80-10-10 Diet" for that accurate designation by the way)*

I didn't eat anything much different than I'd already been eating, just larger volumes.

I kept this up all the way through college. The food changed a little in college because I got obsessed with Black and White cookies, egg and cheese sandwiches, and shrimp salad. Most days I'd eat at least four giant black and whites, two egg and cheese on a roll with lots of ketchup, a shrimp salad sandwich before I left the university, and a whole box of pasta with a whole can of parmesan cheese *(and a whole jar of tomato sauce)* for dinner.

I stayed thin throughout college, and I never threw up to undo the damage. I just worked out like crazy.

In order to stop overeating, I had to stop thinking about these as "the good old days." I couldn't keep romanticizing and wishing I still had the time and physiology to process all that junk. I had to start thinking about it as "the bad old days" ...before I realized the potential I had to live my life, be a leader, connect with other people, and experience everything the world and nature had to offer WITHOUT overeating. *(Thanks to Jack Trimpey, author of "Rational Recovery" for this insight.)*

What are your personal 'bad old days?' How will you remember to think of them as such?

Meeting the Woman I Would Marry

I first met my ex-wife when I was 17 years old, smack in the middle of the birth of my Super Pig. She recalls our first meeting to have been in the kitchen, where I was eating a big jar of peanut butter with a spoon. My ex always said I looked like Superman eating peanut butter that day, and she fell in love with me instantly.

I recall, however, first crushing on her at one of the group therapy marathons that year when she walked into the room with a BIG bag of cherry Danishes and proceeded to eat all of them, one by one...without one shred of guilt or shame. It turns out there was a kind of abusive story about her father surrounding her interaction with the cherry Danishes in their deli when she was little. It's a long story, but she'd decided it was therapeutic for her to eat a whole bag in front of everyone... and I kind of admired that at the time.

I guess peanut butter and cherry Danishes were perhaps NOT the world's best thing to base a marriage on, but that IS how it all started. You might say my Pig fell in love with her Pig. In fact, you should, because that was a big part of it, at least from my perspective.

There were good things though. The first five years of our marriage were an exciting time. We were in love. My ex helped me try things I'd never have had the nerve to try on my own, like writing proposals for big companies, etc. She also supported me through graduate school and for that I'll be forever grateful.

But, in my opinion, our Pigs supported each other, and both of our eating problems prevailed in ways I'm not sure they would have on their own.

Given that we're now divorced, and out of respect for the 28 years we were married, I'm not going to detail much more about my relationship with Sharon. I'll only say this: We always conflicted about dietary philosophies, and this made it more difficult to eat well, I think for both of us. That's not why we got divorced, but it was a strain on the relationship.

My ex believed in a low carbohydrate, high fat, meat-based diet, whereas I believed in a high carbohydrate, low fat, plant-based diet. I'm oversimplifying things, and there were years when we tried to meet in the middle, but it was very difficult.

Today I believe, with Never Binge Again in your pocket, it's possible to live with someone who not only eats exactly the opposite from your dietary philosophy, but constantly puts the most tempting Slop in your face *(which my ex did NOT do.)* That said, if you have a choice, it's a LOT easier when the person you love eats somewhat like you do. Part of wanting to be intimate with someone is a merging of beliefs about primitive values like "how we feed ourselves in this family." You can fight it and win for sure, but it's another one of those things that makes life very uncomfortable. It's different with friends, clients, and other loved ones—but with a spouse and/or very significant other, there's a constant tension when you eat differently. It's just the way it is.

If you DO live with a food-challenging significant other, the trick is to articulate FOR YOURSELF (not out loud and/or

with your partner) exactly what your Food Plan is, and exactly why you believe in YOUR dietary philosophy. You've got to do a little more thinking work. You've got to identify the specific temptations your partner presents you with that tend to trouble you. And it's helpful if you can logically disempower them, then find a way to expose yourself to that information repeatedly until the temptation to give in to your partner is gone.

For example, I was never tempted by the meat my ex ate so often. But I was tempted by the idea of eating more healthy fat, even though personally my research led me to the conclusion you could get all the healthy fat you needed on a plant-based diet if you had one or two avocados per week. Eating lots of nuts and seeds weren't necessary... and in fact would keep me a lot heavier than I wanted to be.

So I did some research and determined that excess fat in the diet can interfere with the functioning of the cells which produce a compound known as Nitric Oxide (NO). NO is a vasodilator which relaxes and opens the blood vessels and lowers blood pressure. Besides assisting in preventing heart attacks and strokes, it can also prevent erectile dysfunction later in life...

That little bit of information helped me pass on the cashews, thank you very much!

In any case, my ex and I were good friends from 1981 to 1987 when she finally divorced her previous husband. She'd try to help me with my girlfriends, and I'd try to help her with the issues in her marriage. But once she was free, we got together very quickly, and married ten months later, in March of '88.

I think things started to deteriorate about five years thereafter when she realized I wasn't open to having a baby unless she stopped traveling so much for business. We both wanted children, but we had a serious misunderstanding. I think she thought I'd be willing to sacrifice my career and become a "Mr.

Mom" ... or else just pay an Au Pair to raise the child. Or launch myself full force into the corporate consulting which paid MUCH better than clinical psychology did.

I wasn't willing to do either of the first two things, and I wasn't built for a full-time career in corporate consulting. *("I'm a lover, not a fighter.")* My ex was significantly older than me, so we didn't have decades to figure out another solution.

Once it became clear children weren't in the picture, things started to deteriorate in many of the ways most familiar to me as a couple's therapist. Communications failed, then the cuddling diminished greatly. Then there was the serious business failure *(and near bankruptcy)* I mentioned earlier, which really put the kibosh on any remaining romance we had because we seriously disagreed about how to handle that too.

We hung in another 15 years, living progressively more like brother and sister...until the trust finally eroded. We're not friends now, and probably never will be... but we're not enemies either. We wish each other well.

My First Car

My parents bought me a 1982 Honda Accord with a hatchback when I was 17, the day after I wrecked their Mercedes on a date with the only girl I had the courage to ask out in high school. I thought that was a strange message, but I was NOT going to complain. I think Dad wanted to reward me for trying with that girl.

In any case, with the car came mobility, and with mobility came the ability to drive places and buy more Pig Slop, though of course I didn't call it that back then. Remember, this was just after I'd discovered the exercise trick, so you'd better believe I drove around. NOTHING was off my Food Plan as long as I worked out hard enough, and I was able to remain thin. Despite this, I mostly just took my friends to the diner to get enormous muffins and gobs of coffee. And went out for pizza.

But something else changed with the introduction of my own car...

I had a PLACE to eat in private. And I took advantage!

What was also new about having my own car is that I had a place I wasn't required to clean up...and I developed a very bad habit: I'd throw all the empty wrappers in the back. Before you knew it, the back was totally filled with garbage. The more wrappers which accumulated, the more resistant I felt about cleaning up. My friends thought it was funny, but I actually thought it was gross... I just couldn't get myself to take care of it.

In my contemporary life I've discovered thoroughly cleaning my car inside and out is a great way to keep me motivated and on track with my eating. It's also a great thing for me to do if, perchance, I do make a mistake with food *(which I never will again!)* There's something about a clean car, and the act of cleaning the car, which now signals to me that I care about myself, and more importantly, that the days of the hatchback-full-of-garbage are behind me. In the days when I still actually binged, I even found cleaning the car was a great way to END the binge.

Pause for a moment here and ask yourself what YOUR personal signals are that you care about yourself? Do you have any memories associated with this? Something you can leave behind you with a real, physical signal in your modern environment?

Oh – there's one more thing about the car. I don't recall this myself, but my sister says I always kept chocolate fudge frosted Pop-Tarts in the glove compartment. Makes sense to me. *(For what it's worth, my sister and I also buried a time machine in the front yard when we were little. Guess what we put in there?)*

CHAPTER 6: MY 20S – THE PIG TAKES HOLD

Starting Graduate School

My mid-twenties were the time when I first started to feel like my eating was a problem. Up until then I managed to stay successfully thin, but really, I was just a great big eating, exercising, sleeping, and pooping machine. Once I entered graduate school though, I couldn't stay thin anymore. Things were a LOT different...

First, college had been a piece of cake. I went to a state school—Stony Brook University in New York. I hardly had to study at all to get straight A's. It only cost about $3,500 per year at the time.

Graduate school was an entirely different animal, however.

I was exceptionally motivated to be a great psychologist, not just casually breeze through and hang out with friends like I did in college. I'd worked exceptionally hard to get into one of the top schools in the country—*Yeshiva University on the Einstein Medical Campus*—and I'd been accepted to six other prestigious schools too. Most people don't know that Ph.D. programs in psychology are harder to get into than medical school. I was very proud of myself, and I really wanted to shine...

But I didn't. At least not right away.

When I got to graduate school what I discovered was that I was one of about 30 people who'd also been at the top of their class.

I'd jumped through so many hurdles that I suddenly found myself competing with the best of the best, and it was stressful. The reading load was, I perceived, inhuman. The onslaught of assignments and homework were way beyond anything I was used to. And the caliber of discussion in class was so much higher than I'd been accustomed to that I really struggled to keep up at first.

I felt like a fish out of water.

And I could NOT afford to keep eating like I was because there was no time to exercise and sleep it off...but I kept at it anyway.

It was probably at this point that I learned what Jack Trimpey terms as "addiction expanding to the tolerance that surrounds it." In other words, my Pig would get away with as much as it possibly COULD get away with. I didn't conceptualize it this way at the time, but I was letting my Pig push my misery level as high as I could possibly tolerate despite the fact my life circumstances were clearly indicating it was time to stop... just so it could maximize it's pleasure.

In the 12 step programs they talk about this concept as "finding your bottom." They might tell you that you have to do "more research" or that you haven't "hit bottom" yet...

But did you ever stop to think that framing it that way is a way to maximize the Pig's time in control? It's like saying "You're suffering? Too bad, so sad. You'll have to suffer a LOT more before your Pig finally makes you sick and tired of being sick and tired. You're not at your bottom yet. Keep binging – Yippee!!"

YOU DO NOT HAVE TO HIT BOTTOM TO STOP OVEREATING. You do NOT have to subject your body to as much abuse as it can humanly tolerate. You do NOT have to wait until you get diabetes, a heart attack, stroke, or until some other horrible health problem visits you. You do NOT have to wait until your loved one leaves you. Your body is NOT a big Pig's Trough and/ or garbage can meant to be stuffed with as much Slop as pos-

sible until it can't take one more drop...

YOU CAN STOP OVEREATING RIGHT NOW EVEN IF YOU ARE PERFECTLY HEALTHY AND FULL OF ENERGY. You can live by the principle of maximizing your health and presence in life vs. your Pig's principle of maximizing immediate gratification at any cost. You can treat your body like a sacred vessel. YOU are in control and YOU can choose. *(Read that again please.)*

I wish I knew this in 1987 when I was starting graduate school. I don't know why it's not a more prevalent idea in our culture. Why isn't anyone talking about this?

Sadly, I lived by the "find your bottom" principle for another 20 years. And my bottom was a LOT further down than I'd ever imagined ☹

My Biggest Regret

Within a few months after I was married, we'd purchased a house in Bayville, Long Island.

This was one of the stupidest moving decisions of my life. Bayville was a gorgeous town situated on the north shore, and it was incredibly beautiful, but I was going to school in the Bronx! I had morning classes which put me smack in the middle of rush hour. And anyone who knows the geography of NYC and the surrounding area knows this was a nightmare drive. "Pray for me, I drive the Long Island Expressway" is the standing joke. You'll even see it on bumper stickers. It took at least two hours in traffic both ways.

But hey, at least I had my car ride to shovel in the Slop.

Later, in my thirties, I'd learn to listen to audio books whenever I was stuck in the car for long stretches. I found that if I fed my mind, my urge to binge eat would often recede. Audio books (and books in general) have always been a salvation for me. They make me feel inspired when my Pig makes me feel hopeless.

Learn something. Know something. It's not only inspiring, but a real competitive advantage in this world. And it engages your neocortex—the upper part of your brain responsible for your human identity and delaying gratification in pursuit of long-term goals and dreams. The urge to overeat is driven by lower parts of the brain... those more primitively evolved which are more interested in fight or flight, feast or famine, eat, mate, or kill. Anything you can do to jump back up into the higher part of your brain at the moment of impulse can help!

This is why I'm also dedicated to getting as many of my books into Audible as possible. At the time of this publication only Never Binge Again was available in audio format (get it here https://www.audible.com/pd/B01GP0MXDU/?source_code=AUDFPWS0223189MWT-BK-ACX0-060653&ref=acx_bty_BK_ACX0_060653_rh_us) **but check back frequently and you're likely to find the rest!** *(My other books include "45 Binge Trigger Busters" and "The Food Demon Interviews")*

Pause here to ask how you might feed your mind in ways that could conceivably mitigate your cravings for Slop please?

In any case, I mostly wasted my commuting time in graduate school eating Pig Slop and listening to Howard Stern. I wish I could get that time back.

Moving on, the wedding itself created a lot trouble...

My parents disapproved of our age difference, as well as the fact my ex was one of my Dad's patients. I guess I forgot to mention that part. I was a bad boy! I think the whole family had something to do with setting that up... everything from the fact it wasn't totally clear whether I was a therapist in training in the practice vs. another patient participating, to my parents having never said anything nice about any of the women I dated in high school or college, to Mom and Dad still dealing with a lot of tension between themselves as a result of their open marriage. *(They divorced a few years later)*.

But in the end, I knew I wasn't supposed to kiss anyone from the practice, much less sleep with them, so I was definitely being a bad boy!

Mom screamed at me whenever we spoke. More than that, she said very foul things about what my ex and I must be doing together sexually. It became untenable to be in the same room with Mom, or even talk on the telephone.

Dad was a lot more rational but didn't feel he could give me all the reasons he felt I shouldn't marry my ex, because he owed her confidentiality due to their previous relationship. What he did tell me was that she wasn't really in love with ME, but that transference was strongly at play from HIS therapeutic relationship with her. *(He had to be at least partially right, but I also think we had something real, at least for the first few years. And Dad didn't run a traditional psychoanalytic practice with traditional boundaries, so a lot of that just didn't apply. Things were all mixed up.)*

My sister just politely told me my ex was not the person to fall in love with in the practice. She pointed to another woman I was very close to and said "why don't you consider her instead?"

The thing of it is, they were ALL correct, but I just couldn't see it.

And so, what I did next was just awful...

After inviting my parents *(and my sister)* to the wedding...

Making a deposit on the hall...

And having both my family AND my ex's family say they couldn't make the date...

My ex and I called a justice of the peace over to the house spontaneously one evening and got married with just one witness...

AND STOPPED TALKING TO MY FAMILY ENTIRELY.

It took two years before Dad, Laurie, and I reconnected, and four years before I reconnected with my mother. But even then, the relationship with my parents was very strained for decades. My relationship with Laurie got better a lot more quickly, but there was damage done there too.

Looking back on things, I know I didn't have the psychological strength and skills to manage the situation in a more mature way when it first went down. I forgive myself for it, and my family forgave me long ago. But I DEEPLY regret the ensuing rift I allowed to fester for decades.

I was particularly filled with regret when Mom died in 2017, and I realized we'd only had the five or six years before her death to connect in earnest. I missed out on a lifetime with a wonderful woman, and I caused her great pain.

At least we had those last few years. And at least the insight has propelled me to value family on a much deeper level than I ever did before. My dad will be 81 years old this spring, and he's still going strong. I make sure to talk to him a few times per week and visit a few times per year. We're both very happy about the renewed warmth and vigor in the relationship.

Looking back, I now also know that a big part of what allowed me to maintain the distance was my over-involvement with Slop. My obsession with binge eating ensured I barely had the energy to manage my career and finances. I didn't have the emotional presence and/or mental energy to repair these relationships, even though I did acquire the skills as the years went by. Remember, I'm a highly trained psychologist!

And this, much more so than my failed marriage, and more so than many failures along the way in my career, is the most painful thing in my life. It's my biggest regret. There was nothing worse than the moment I saw my mother in her casket and thought "I'm sorry Mom, I let you down. I was eating a bunch of chocolate and pizza when I should've been returning the love you gave me as a child."

I do take solace in the fact that if there is an afterlife, Mom forgives me, I know. She knows she was less than perfect, and I sure know that about myself. We apologized to one another in her final few years. But I'll tell you what, I'll be damned if I'm ever going to let a chocolate bar steal even one more precious moment from a treasured relationship in my life again! I am here to connect, love, teach, and learn...NOT to become a big eating, exercising, sleeping, and pooping machine!

Here's an exercise you can do right now to leverage this insight in YOUR life. Take a moment and think of the person you love most. Now, assume you were going to allow yourself to just let go and binge eat for ten years. Go ahead and write that person an apology letter to explain why you chose overeating over your connection to them. Tell them why Pig Slop was more important than the love you might've shared over that decade. See if you can find even one good reason which might be acceptable to them... and to you. You can't, can you? This is a very powerful exercise. Keep the letter and read it over daily for a month, and then again any time you need motivation to stay on (or get back on) track.

Thanks to John Chancellor, one of my most treasured mentors for giving me this idea. You can hear the interview where it first arose on my podcast here: https://www.neverbingeagain.com/TheBlog/uncategorized/stop-overeating-by-writing-a-letter-to-your-future-self/ *(And you can find more of John's work at www.TeachTheSoul.com)*

During graduate school, given the commute, I really couldn't do much else career wise, besides organizing the finances and running the books for my ex's business. Food throughout my early to mid-twenties got progressively worse.

My First Patient

What I do very distinctly remember as a transition point in my early twenties was the moment I was to see my very first paying client. First, I recall all the discussions with my peers about how frightening it was to step up and take responsibility in the position of a therapist. Who the hell were we to think we could help other people with their lives?

A LOT of people quit just before facing that moment. I've come to find out that's a very common thing in graduate schools for psychology. Same thing for coaches.

It's kind of terrifying in theory, but once you've done your first few sessions it's not so bad. I'd liken it to jumping into a pool full of cold water from a ten-foot diving board. If you know how to swim even semi-decently, you're going to be fine once you jump in, but that first step's a doozy!

My first patient was a homosexual man in his early sixties. He came in because he was feeling unhappy in his primary relationship. On the telephone he said he craved more emotional intimacy with his partner.

I'll never forget how he presented, because as he walked in the door, he handed me a plate of cheeseballs and a box of condoms. "I brought you a present to start things off right", he said with a smile on his face.

Now, where the heck is the textbook which tells you what to do in THAT situation?

I didn't handle it well...

I said something like "I'm not sure that's an appropriate gift for me to accept. We're supposed to do everything in words here, you see."

Technically that was correct, but it didn't address his deepest need, and it was WAY too judgmental and procedural for the initial interaction. His deepest need was to zero in on the dynamics which were preventing him from achieving the emotional intimacy he wanted with his partner. What I should've said was "What do you think about the notion of sex against intimacy?"

Now, you may be thinking "OK, so what does this have to do with overcoming overeating?"

Everything.

The success of my psychology practice is largely due, from the moment of my first client interaction forward, to my willingness to ask "What should I have done? What would I do differently next time?"

That moment was just one of literally thousands of moments with clients that I analyzed. In every session with every patient I found there was something I wish I'd done differently. I talked to supervisors. I read books. I got outside perspectives. And the whole time I wasn't beating myself up, I was instead just asking "What could I have done differently? What might I want to do next time?"

I want you to know I wasn't just a little successful in my psychology practice either. I was extraordinarily successful. Like the kind of success that turned the heads of ALL my peers. In the middle of the 1990s when all my peers were complaining about how the insurance industry and managed care was ruining the profession, I got literally hundreds of private pay clients. Couples who came to see me almost never got divorced. Suicidal clients never suicided. Zero. And I was earning a full time, private income in under one year's time.

I think you see where I'm going.

What your Pig wants you to do when you make a mistake is focus on everything you did wrong, not what you could do better. It wants you to feel pathetic. It wants you to feel too weak to resist the next overeating episode. But You can choose other-wise. You can look at every mistake as a learning experience, and make sure you get the most out of it. That sounds trite, but it makes all the difference.

I once had dinner with a multimillionaire. He made his money selling a subscription service at seminars. I asked him what the best thing he ever learned was and he said *"You know, Glenn, you might not believe me, but my wife and I had this notebook. And after every single seminar we sat down and asked ourselves 'What went right and how can we emphasize that more next time?' Then we asked 'What went wrong and how might we do it better next time?' We reviewed that book before each new seminar and made the changes. You wouldn't believe how fast we got better, and how quickly the money started rolling in."*

"Success is not final, failure is not fatal: it is the courage to continue that counts" - Winston Churchill

"Success is going from failure to failure without losing your enthusiasm." - Winston Churchill

CHAPTER 7: MY 30S – FALLING DOWN AND GETTING BACK UP AGAIN

The years 1994 through 2004, from roughly my 30th birthday until my 40th, were characterized by building successes which were either torn down by outside forces, or which I chose to tear down myself. In retrospect, although it seemed like I was making good decisions every step of the way, and although I experienced successes most people only dream of during these periods, I now believe I was repeating the experience of having lost everything during the most difficult period of my childhood—the years from 9 to 14 when my family came apart, and my grandparents were jettisoned from the house.

In some way, I couldn't let myself continue to build on anything meaningful and secure, because I hadn't experienced the continued building of meaning and security in my foundation. Of course, there was more to it than that. I was too smart for my own good. I believed I could succeed at ANYTHING I wanted, and I'd largely proven myself right. Therefore, there was no good reason to get "stuck" in any one endeavor, or so I thought. So, I kept jumping around.

Plus, except for brief respites when I'd work hard with one eating disorders specialist or another *(or during my time in Over-*

eaters Anonymous), my overeating was getting worse during my 30s, and so was my weight.

Food kept me from truly understanding what I was doing. Food kept me from reaching my true potential and helping as many people as I otherwise could have.

Pause here to ask yourself what your food obsession might have taken from you?

My Clinical Practice

In my early 30s I focused on building a child and family practice. It was exceptionally meaningful, though not nearly as lucrative as my corporate consulting had been. My days were filled with challenge, people, and purpose. I learned more and got better every day. Working with clients was what I was built for in so many ways.

People often ask if I worked with eating disordered clients during this time. The answer is definitively NO!

After seeing just a few people seriously struggling with food in the very beginning of my practice, I realized it was hypocritical of me to try and help them myself when I had such a big problem with my own eating. I specialized in working with couples and families. If one member of the couple had an eating problem, I might keep working with them on their couples' issues, but I'd refer them to a specialist to help with food.

Even though, to this day I am exceptionally proud of the practice I built—*the memories are among my fondest*—I could have done a LOT better if it weren't for my food obsession. You just can't be 100% present when all you can think about is getting to the pizza place while you're sitting with a suicidal patient. And you can't process everything afterwards in the way you need to when you're sitting on the couch and sweating, having eaten a whole pizza...

Thank God I never lost anyone.

In 2001, I decided I needed to help my ex-wife with the focus group facility we'd invested so heavily in. I therefore told my patients I was taking a sabbatical from my practice for a year, and that was my intention. But I never went back to full time practice again. Sometimes, clients from almost 20 years ago still call to update me and/or request a phone session. To this day it amazes me the depth of connection you form when you do therapy the right way.

The Fortune 500 Consulting Business

Simultaneous to developing my clinical practice, I also started doing a lot more advertising consulting for the Fortune 500 companies I mentioned in the beginning of the book. See, in graduate school I'd learned a type of study design and statistical analysis which allowed me to quantify psychological reactions without having to ask direct questions. I developed an extremely desirable protocol for very specific advertising tasks. It could assess the emotional values associated with purchase interest for specific products and services WITHOUT running the risk of "social desirability bias" (not providing genuine answers due to fear of looking bad to others). No other protocol in the global market research at the time could match its power and statistical purity.

I LOVED the work. Designing, running, and interpreting the studies was fascinating. But I hated the corporate politics, and most of the clients I worked for were in Big Food and/or Big Pharma, so I felt guilty about the products I was helping them put out into the world. That said, there were a few projects where everything came together without guilt (for Whirlpool for example) and they made me the happiest.

In 1998 we (my ex-wife and I through our company) were paid approximately $1,000,000 by a major vision-care company to organize and execute a global study based on this protocol. To that point I'd never written a proposal for more than $100,000 and had never done anything internationally.

It was thrilling! And f-----king terrifying.

I remember seeing the request-for-proposal and saying to my ex "There's NO reason we can't do this. There's nothing they are requesting which we can't solve. It's just like doing 7 studies, about the size we are already used to executing, but all simultaneously and putting it together." So, I bit the bullet and wrote the proposal. After a few rounds of questions, they said "OK, send us an invoice." So, I wrote my bookkeeper an email and said something like "Can you create an invoice for $250,000 deposit for XYZ company on ABC job... and send it out right way please?" She called me to double check the number, said OK, and a few weeks later we had the money.

It was a crazy, exciting time. I quickly had to get up to speed on how international studies were conducted. I learned how to translate my work to six different languages since the study involved 2,000 patients and 600 doctors in eight different countries. USA, France, Germany, the United Kingdom, Singapore, China, Japan, and Brazil. I decided that because I'd charged such a high price, I'd just hire subcontractors for everything I could and let them teach me how to do it.

The skill of translating my work to multiple languages proved very useful for Never Binge Again, where we are now in process of translation to Spanish, Italian, German, Hebrew, Greek, and more. The key turns out to be having the book translated BACK to English after it's translated to a foreign language. That's how you can really spot troubled areas in the translation. I'd have had no idea about this if I hadn't done this proposal.

Learning to manage high-cost, high-end contractors around the globe shouldn't be discounted either. This was my first experience understanding what you could really accomplish if you were willing to step up and be a leader. That skill would later serve me when I developed an advertising agency which grew to have dozens of employees and interns and helps me to this day in my current company.

In any case, that entire year was wild. Remember, I was still seeing a full practice of patients, and my ex was still flying around for other corporate consulting projects. We had to handle this on TOP of everything else.

At one-point things were REALLY falling apart in China and Japan. The subcontractors didn't understand the protocol, and it wasn't working to talk to them on the telephone and internet. I really had to be with them to show them how it was done. Or at least, that was my strong perception. Remember, this was 1998, internet video conferencing capability was ancient and slow!

So, right in the middle of a full week of suicidal patients, I figured out how to get everyone to fly to the airport in Tokyo for a one-hour meeting. I literally got on a plane in NYC, flew 14 hours to Japan, had a one-hour meeting, and got on a plane two hours later to come home. It did the trick. *(There's a funny story about my not having had the time to study Japanese culture before I left. Apparently, I didn't do something correctly to formally release the subcontractors from their social obligations. They insisted on buying me dinner, and everyone ordered EXACTLY what I did. All 18 people in attendance. Then they followed me to the bathroom bowing and bowing at me until I finally walked into the toilet and closed the door. Guess I didn't get the right memo on that one.)*

In the end, the project went well, and the client was happy, but they decided not to take our advice. We wound up with about $300,000 net profit, and it was the first time in my life I'd had that kind of reserve. I felt exceptionally proud.

There are two major takeaways you can glean from this experience:

> **FIRST, YOU CAN DO A LOT MORE THAN YOU THINK YOU CAN DO.** It's only because I was willing to step WAY out of my comfort zone that I could pull off this million-dollar project. I had a vague sense, intellectually, that there was nothing about managing an international study like this which I wouldn't be able to handle, and that I'd be able to pay people to teach me everything I didn't know... but I was FAR from knowledgeable about every step of the process. I trusted my gut and said "YES I CAN DO IT" anyway, and I turned out to be right. I COULD have flopped, but it was my risk to take. What's yours?

> **SECOND: When you take risks outside your comfort zone, you pick up skills which will serve you in all sorts of ways you could never have planned for, or even known would be useful**.

Your Pig doesn't want you to take risks because that could result in you growing and feeling you have more purpose and skills suitable for life, which would make binging seem infinitely less interesting.

The Financial Disaster

With several hundred thousand dollars in the bank from the big project ending in the fall of '99, we decided we finally had the cushion we needed to switch sides of the industry. That was desirable because the other side of the industry didn't have to travel, only organize and care for the research participants.

So we decided to build the biggest, fanciest, most technologically advanced focus group facility you could imagine. We spared no expense (despite my urging) and before we knew it we were committed to about $150,000 per month in expenses, with only $60,000 of income coming from it at the beginning. Can you say "Ouch!?"

We had to make up the deficit by doing more corporate consulting projects. We sold another $500,000 or so using the protocol above with other companies. That was a blast too.

But thereafter my ability to get along with my ex on a project seriously deteriorated due to a major disagreement about how we were SPENDING the profit from the first project. See, we launched the focus group facility in 2001, not long before 9/11 hit. As we were just outside NYC, the odds of corporations wanting to fly their people to do research in New York were slim to none. I knew that on September 12th and begged my ex to close shop. We were dead in the water and, despite marketing very hard (*I started a newsletter and was prolific with it – that's where we got all the new clients*), I saw NO way we'd be able to weather the storm.

But my ex refused to close. She wanted to put everything into the business. She said this was her "baby".

In any event, we held onto the research facility for two more years while going very deep into debt. The $500,000 of additional consulting money from those projects just got poured into the new business as I watched everything go downhill. I slowly withdrew from the corporate consulting at this time, and in the end, we owed $700,000 and spent the next 6 years paying it back.

As I mentioned previously, I overate my way through all this stress. I ballooned up to a kind of awful looking version of myself. It looked like someone had eaten Glenn.

I was furious. And because I'd had a very bad car accident, the stress was a particularly terrible additional burden. I wound up living with severe migraines more days than not, and by 2003 I was just barely working. Even when I started to recover in earnest from my eating troubles, it took me several years to get back to the healthy version of myself again.

There are several things you can take away from this horrible experience:

➢ **As mentioned previously, I got fat, sick, and broke, when I could've just been broke.** There's NEVER a good reason to overeat. It's ALWAYS better to be present in the moment and deal with reality. It takes a long time to claw your way back from digging a big hole. So, if you're in a hole, stop digging!

➢ **The bottom is a LOT further down than you think it is.** I couldn't believe how long it was possible to work with vendors whom I owed tens of thousands of dollars... as long as I didn't dodge their calls. Nobody showed up in a white suit with a mustache to take away my car, computer, house, or even my office lease. This gave me a newfound confidence in business I'd never experienced to that point.

➢ **You can dig your way out of even the deepest hole if your time horizon is long enough.**

There are almost no pictures I saved of myself during this time. I'd ballooned to approximately 280 pounds. I say approximately, because I stopped weighing myself at 257... but I kept eating and gaining so this is probably a conservative estimate.

CHAPTER 8: MY 40S –THINKING ABOUT WHAT MONEY REALLY MEANS AND DISCOVERING NATURE AGAIN

http://www.neverbingeagain.com/images/GlennAbout43.jpg

It was in my early 40s, roughly around the same time I realized we were eventually going to get out of debt, that I discovered the dual-minded nature of addiction and began experimenting with different methods and rules for overcoming overeating using it. I'd read Rational Recovery by Jack Trimpey, done a large study with 40,000 people on the relationship of emotional conflict to specifically preferred junk food, and did a lot of thinking about what I learned in all the consulting I'd done for the food industry.

Taken together, this finally flipped the paradigm with which I approached binge eating. I recognized I had to dominate these urges like an alpha wolf dominates challengers for leadership in the pack – NOT like a loving mother nurturing her wounded child back to health.

In short, I finally got it right and began my recovery in earnest. It's no wonder then, that as I stopped overeating, I started using my mental energy for much more productive purposes, and had some very significant insights, mostly about the meaning of money. In this section, I'd like to share those insights with you.

The overriding insight is this: How you feel about money has very much to do with how you feel about being FED in the world. Money is a symbolic representation of your ability to feed yourself. Improve your relationship with money and your relationship with food can't help but come along.

NOTE: In the final chapter of the book I'll detail the evolution of my successful diet, which also occurred in my 40s, in tandem with the development of the principles in Never Binge Again. I felt it deserved its own chapter rather than just being presented chronologically.

The Strange Psychology of Money

In my 40s, after having recovered from $700,000 of debt, and developing a following of over 30,000 entrepreneurs, I spent a lot of time thinking about what money really meant. Below is an essay I wrote when I was about 44 which summarized a lot of my conclusions. It was VERY well received at the time. I know it helped a lot of people. At minimum, it helped me! I hope it helps you too.

THE VERY STRANGE PSYCHOLOGY OF MONEY

I woke up deep in thought today, reflecting once again on the last 15 years as the year draws to a close. On my mind in particular was this very strange thing we call money, which in and of itself is nothing more than an idea, yet the mere idea of money consumes our lives, inflicts pain, brings joy, and moves people to coordinate their energies and work together towards a common good (or evil).

At this point in my life I've seen both sides of money. I've never been fabulously wealthy, but I've been way WAY above average–AND–as close to bankruptcy as any man can claim without filing.

I've consulted for large corporations who write six figure checks without batting an eye and worked with patients for whom my six-dollar session fee *(at the earliest point in my career)* meant skipping lunch that day.

I have friends who are multi-gazillionaires, and those who could care less about their bank account as long they have a roof over their head, food to eat, and people to love. *(Nothing wrong with having BOTH by the way!)*

And since I've been TEACHING marketing and entrepreneurship, I've been privileged to witness students who succeeded beyond what they ever thought was possible. That said, I watched even more stagnate, get in their own way, and suffer.

So I felt inspired this morning to begin a series on the strange psychology of money... the insights which hide beneath the surface, preventing most of us from getting what we really want in life, which, in my estimation, is not money itself, but the things which money empowers us to do, be, and feel.

I thought I'd start out with a personal observation to get us all going, but I'd be VERY interested in hearing what you all think below. I'll follow up with more later this week.

It's NOT Really Money That We Want

Now, before you yell at me, please know I realize when you don't have enough money to pay the bills, it's hard to want anything else. I'm not sitting here in some lofty castle, and I HAVE felt the personal sting of debt up to my eyeballs.

I also don't want you to get the wrong idea. I really DO like money. In fact, I LOVE money, and I'd like you to give me some today please so I can give you more value. That's the way it's supposed to work, right? Why do we all feel so guilty about saying so? In fact, I think feeling guilty about asking for money is tantamount to saying you don't have value to offer... something to think about, don't you think?

In the end, you see, I don't think it's really the money we want!

If you ARE having trouble paying your bills, ask yourself what you plan to do when you CAN pay them. THAT's what you really want.

Here's where this really hit home for me. When I was deep in debt and on the verge of bankruptcy, I embraced the classic goal-setting literature (Stephen Covey, Brian Tracy, Jim Rohn, etc). I worked very hard on articulating both long-term and short-term goals, attaching pictures to them, writing an overall vision statement, prioritizing it all, and then isolating my single most important mission in life.

Initially that goal was to amass a large sum of money. Very large. Because I couldn't see how I could possibly accomplish all my other goals without it. Even health and relationship goals seemed to pale in comparison, as crazy as that sounds coming from a psychologist. THAT is what soul-crushing debt can do to you. It's easy to SAY we should put health and relationships before money. Indeed, EVERYONE knows you should. But how many of us, especially on the brink of financial ruin, actually DO prioritize health and relationships first? Be honest.

Well, in order to really "stamp in the blueprint" into my psychology, I decided I was going to write out all my goals 10 times each day, in the exact prioritized order, and the do some free-associative journaling to identify obstacles and opportunities.

The strangest thing happened. At first, the financial goal seemed like it really DID belong in first position. After all, the wolves were at the door, we were firing employees left and right, borrowing as much as we possibly could (not only from banks but from friends and family), and barely sleeping.

But one day I noticed that the goals refused to stay in the "right" order in my memory. Some of the health and relationship goals were moving up the list, and I simply couldn't recall the others until I went back and looked where I'd written them down previously. It got to the point that I had to go back to that document repeatedly because no matter how hard I tried, I couldn't finish the list, even though I'd written it out a hundred times.

As this was happening (over the course of a few months), it started to occur to me that I could easily accomplish a lot of these other goals no matter how much debt I had. Climbing mountains, eating better, spending more time with family, friends, and the dogs, making mastermind connections, getting a coach, etc.

As I started doing these things, I found I was HAPPY despite continuing to deal with the debt—which was STILL the pull-the-blanket-over-your-head-and-cry-yourself-to-sleep kind-of debt at the time! Maybe happier than I'd ever been previously.

Finally, one day I noticed I'd written ALL the other goals BEFORE the financial goal, and paradoxically, THAT'S when things started getting better. I think that's because when I really took care of myself body, mind, and soul, then and only then could I put ALL the pieces together for my business.

Now, you might think this story ends with me dropping my financial goals entirely, just "letting go", and "going with the flow", or some such nonsense. Not so. Like I said, I LOVE money, and I'm continuing on with my well-orchestrated and methodical quest to get wealthy.

What's different now is I no longer love money for money's sake. It's not this kind of vague, magical, mysterious and frightening force in my life who's only purpose is to beat down the wolves at the door.

It's something which empowers me to do what I want to do, add value in the way I want to add value, enjoy life in the way I want to enjoy life. Which I think is the highest and best use of money.

I think when we crave money, get obsessed with it, and come to believe it's the ONLY thing which can make our lives better, we're actually expressing a deep fear of money. And if we're frightened of money, we're ever so much more unlikely to allow it into our lives, don't you think?

More simply...

Money obsession is really a hidden financial fear, and financial fear repels money.

Does that make sense? (Do you agree?)

Last, I'm not perfect by any stretch of the imagination, and I still AM occasionally prone to retreating to a fearful, money obsessed state when I get a big tax bill, when we expand any of our businesses with more employees to reach "the next level", when the economy tanks, and even, believe it or not, when I experience a mini-windfall. *(As an aside I've always found it relatively easy to do very big things in the world, but extremely hard to get wealthy doing them.)*

But these feelings are always temporary now, and far, far less intense than ever before.

Because I've learned I can get what's MOST important to me almost entirely without money. Which paradoxically has freed me to make more, and help others do the same.

Please note I made this leap BEFORE the money started coming in.

If we only associate money with fear (even if it's removing fear), I think we're unlikely to ever have much. Do you agree?

I'd like to leave you with one more thought before you leave this essay...

No matter how much you may THINK a craving for Pig Slop is real, I assure you that the Pig Slop is NOT what you really want. There is something underneath it, a more authentic need. A craving for Pig Slop is always a shallow distraction, NOT the real goal. You don't have to believe me, you only need to carefully think what the real craving may be and try various things, no matter how much your Pig say the Slop is the only thing which will do it.

Letting the Market Change You as a Person

Below is another teaching article I wrote about money and the meaning of life in my 40s. It was called "Letting the Market Change You as a Person" and it addressed entrepreneurs with the need to research their market. More importantly, it outlined a psychological insight critical for success not only in business, but in life: When you're trying to accomplish something with a group of other people, no matter whether your goal is to influence them to buy something from you or to change their behavior, you need to open up to them enough TO them, and immerse yourself enough WITH them, that you allow yourself to be changed as a person.

LETTING THE MARKET CHANGE YOU AS A PERSON

My #1 money making secret is Research. #2 money making secret is contrarian advice. Know what #3 is? It's "Let the market change you as a person"

Here's why this is so important. Everyone TALKS a good game when it comes to equating marketing with empathy for your prospects and customers. But truly empathizing with another human being means:

> ➤ Making yourself vulnerable...

> Being open minded and willing to change cherished thoughts and long held opinions...

> Letting yourself FEEL the other person's pain, joy, heartbreak, and despair...

> Truly, deeply, and wholeheartedly absorbing their stories and desires into your soul...

It means changing as a person. (Really)

This means that, in at least some small but significant way, you've yielded your ego to the other person, let *your* values and self-identity disintegrate, and then put yourself together again, better and stronger. The psychological term for this is "regression in the service of the ego."

In fact, I only really know that I'm ready to go INTO a new market when I feel that I've been changed as a person. I'll give you a few examples to drive the point home, and I'll show you how this translates into money making marketing insight.

How a scuzzy little rodent made me a better person: I must admit I originally got into the guinea pig market as a purely mercenary marketing experiment (my first successful internet project). I didn't have any long-standing love for the furry little creatures. In fact, I basically thought of them like my mother did - "scuzzy little rodents with hair." *(I brought one home from summer camp when I was nine without telling her... that's when I first heard them characterized in this charming way.)*

But I knew I could never ethically and honestly market guinea pig care books if I held onto those feelings and beliefs, so I got myself a guinea pig *(actually my ex bought it for me as a gift)* and started cuddling and playing with it every day.

But that didn't do it for me. It still seemed a little scuzzy, like a rodent, even though it occasionally made me laugh.

It was only when I started INTERVIEWING guinea pig owners —*as in, you know, actually talking to people on the phone, like we OLD people used to do way back in the dinosaur era before computers*—asking them WHY they wanted a guinea pig in the first place that my feelings started to change. A surprising number of them said something like this "Because I got my little 7-year-old Suzie a hamster last year and it died after just a few months. She was devastated, and it rocked the whole household. I heard Guinea Pigs live longer and I want our family to have a better experience. I want my little one to learn how to nurture and care for another living creature, and to successfully reap the rewards!"

This hit me in the heart. I've got a little nephew who means the world to me. At that time, he was only three. I remember how upset he was when his pet fish died. So, suddenly a guinea pig was no longer a "scuzzy little rodent with hair", and I wasn't an uncaring adult with no use for them. Now the little monsters were a vehicle of love, and a means to help create children who would responsibly pass love on.

What could be more important?

This immediately crystallized the Unique Selling Proposition I'd use to market the book: "Guinea Pig Secrets Which Can DOUBLE Your Guinea Pigs Life!" I only had to seek proof to support it. I had to actually figure out how to double a guinea pig's life!

Thankfully, it wasn't that hard. It turns out there are about a half dozen little known guinea pig care FACTS which can double the average lifespan. *(AS A SIDE NOTE: You'll be amazed just how ignorant the average market is, and how much blatantly wrong conventional wisdom gets passed around without scientific backing. You can almost always find facts to support a better outcome in any market!)*

For example, what you feed your guinea pig, the litter you use,

Glenn Livingston

how you insulate them from stress, etc. CAN double their life expectancy. The real killer, it turns out, was that most veterinarians didn't realize guinea pigs had a different type of bacteria in their gut than cats and dogs. As a result, giving a guinea pig the same antibiotics as you'd give a cat or a dog can easily kill him. So, veterinarians were frequently killing these little pets by accident. Can you imagine!? I went out and recorded a full set of interviews with vets who specialized in working with guinea pigs and other animals that required these special kinds of antibiotics. And thus, the product was born.

Let me template this process so you can repeat it in your market:

1) Dig deep into the market with surveys, research, and other online intelligence.

2) TALK to people. Go out and meet them. LIVE the same problems your market is living

3) Know yourself. Let yourself feel how the market is changing you.

4) When you get "hit in the heart", when a deep feeling of change comes over you, know that you're onto something which is probably the core of what your USP needs to be

5) Formulate your USP

6) Find proof to support it. Intriguingly, there's almost always proof available. The thing is, hardly anyone really digs this deeply in most markets, so there's LOTS of gold available for the taking.

I hope this is getting you to start thinking.

Have you let YOUR market change you?

How, specifically?

You should be able to articulate it in as much detail as I did

106

above. If you can't, it means you need to spend more time IN your market, talking to them, smelling them, living their pain.

Food for thought.

For SERIOUS thought...

Because this applies to your struggles with food too!

See, when you're attempting to overcome overeating and let go of a particular type of trouble food and/or eating behavior, what you're really trying to do is "enter a new market" and connect with a different type of food. In order to do that, you need to let the new food change you as a person. You need to develop a relationship with that new food and understand why people might come to love it, even though your Pig says its utterly unlovable. You need to experience that new food with the totality of your being, let it impact you, let yourself love and be loved by it. You need to let healthy food change you.

This probably involves more fruits and vegetables, but it could be anything.

Let healthy food change you as a person.

Also in my 40s - Discovering Never Binge Again

Perhaps most importantly, it was in my 40s that I discovered the Never Binge Again principles, which are outlined in detail in the FREE book at www.NeverBingeAgain.com , and summarized in 45 Binge Trigger Busters *(www.45BingeTriggers.com)*... so I won't go into detail about the principles themselves here. But briefly:

> ➤ **YOU CAN'T LOVE YOURSELF THIN:** Popular mythology holds that it's not what you're eating, it's what's eating *you* that keeps you overeating. Therefore, the thinking goes, you must learn love yourself and fill that hole in your heart

if you want to stop. Unfortunately, this line of reasoning ignores two critical facts (1) The reptilian brain, that primitive neurological structure most responsible for addiction, doesn't know love – it only knows "eat, mate, or kill"; (2) Industry spends billions of dollars engineering food-like substances to override out best judgment. Then Big Food spends a fortune on Big Advertising to make us believe it too. These very strong forces are at work regardless of how much you love *(or don't love)* yourself, no matter what unresolved trauma you hold in your heart, and no matter how angry, lonely, sad, tired, happy, depressed, and/or anxious you happen to get. Pretend you are an alpha wolf dealing with a challenger for leadership of the pack. Don't love and nurture the challenger, tell it that if it doesn't get back in line, you're going to kill it. *(You can't actually do that, but you can display the intent with an attitude of total superiority and confidence, and it will retreat.)*

➤ **USE HARD AND FAST RULES INSTEAD OF GUIDELINES:** Guidelines require constant decision making about food, and decisions wear down your willpower. The research strongly suggests there are only so many good decisions we can make each day. So, for example, if you say "I'm going to avoid chocolate 90% of the time and eat it 10%," you've put yourself in a very bad position. Now you'll have to make a chocolate decision every time you're in front of a bar at the checkout counter in Starbucks... and that takes a LOT of willpower! In contrast, if you say "I'm only going to eat chocolate on the last three days of the Calendar Month, and never more than 2 oz per Calendar Day" you've effectively accomplished the same 90/10 split *(3 days out of 30 is ten percent)*, except this time all your decisions are already made. No will power needed!

➤ **CULTIVATE CONFIDENCE IN THE FACE OF YOUR IMPULSES, NOT FEAR:** Our culture also widely believes the impulse to overeat is irresistible to certain people in certain situations, and more importantly, that the only way to combat it is to form dependent relationships with accountability partners, rush to support groups, avoid tempting situations, get a sponsor, etc. Some go so far as suggesting overeating must be disease. Never Binge Again doesn't buy into this mythology at all. Instead, we believe the problem is nothing more than a healthy appetite corrupted by industry for profit. Our best defense is to confidently define exactly where the line is between healthy vs. unhealthy eating for ourselves, then listen carefully for that destructive voice within us, and either ignore and/or disempower it while we otherwise thoroughly nourish our bodies. Cultivating a confident attitude helps you develop a success identity, and a success identity is what empowers you to Never Binge Again.

➤ **WELCOME YOUR CRAVINGS DON'T FEAR THEM!** Many people are terrified they'll get an "irresistible" craving, and walk around frightened of their own bodies, feeling like a slave to their own impulses. But that's NO way to live! Never Binge Again asserts we are always in control despite what the Food Industry, the Advertising Industry, the Addiction Treatment Industry, and our Pigs would have us believe. A craving is something to be welcomed. it is only by experiencing your cravings that you get the opportunity to extinguish them. Plus, behind every craving is almost always an authentic need. Something you genuinely do need in order to feed your body or your mind, but profiteers in industry have seduced your survival drive into thinking it needs the wrong thing. You can't possibly "need" that bag of chips right now because there were no chips when we were evolving in the tropics – your body and your brain has made a biological error. Every bone in your body may believe you "need" that bag, box, or container, but feelings aren't facts and you do not need pig slop to survive no matter how much it may feel like you do! seize every craving as an opportunity to extinguish the craving itself, and to actively reprogram your body to crave what it needs instead. Your body will adjust!

> **DON'T HOPE AND PRAY FOR PEACE WITH FOOD – FORCEFULLY DECLARE YOUR RECOVERY INSTEAD**: In twelve step programs people are taught to seek conscious contact with God and pray that He remove their impulse to overeat. They are told they're powerless over their addictions and the best they can do is pray for God to remove their desire to act them out. This is very odd when you think about it. Every major religion suggests that we should behave well in order to please God, not ask God to MAKE us stop behaving badly. And why would God EVER remove the healthy desire to find calories and nutrition from us? Wasn't there a reason He put it there in the first place? I'm admittedly not a religious person or even a scholar of the ancient books, so I'm not prepared to debate this in detail, but something seems very fishy on its surface, don't you think? Even for non-religious people, why would you want to hope and pray for peace with food when you could take control and CREATE it for yourself. **DON'T HOPE AND PRAY FOR PEACE WITH FOOD!** Hoping, wishing, and praying for peace with food is just your Pig saying "Gee, I wish we could be one of the lucky ones - maybe if we hope and pray long enough we will be - but in the meantime you know what will make us feel better? Hmmmmmm??? Do ya? Go get us some Slop!!!" CLAIM your peace with food instead. Declare it. Breathe, then make a 100% commitment to stick to your plan, and recognize that any thought, feeling, image, or impulse suggesting you'll ever break this plan between now and the day you die is Pig Squeal. ALL DOUBT AND UNCERTAINTY IS PIG ACTIVITY. HOPE IS PIG ACTIVITY. Don't hope for it, claim it, know it, be it!

> **COMMIT WITH PERFECTION BUT FORGIVE YOURSELF WITH DIGNITY:** This was the biggest breakthrough insight I had that seriously diverged from Jack Trimpey's Rational Recovery. Rational Recovery is a very similar philosophy to Never Binge Again but focuses largely on drugs and alcohol, which I call the "black and white" addictions —those you can cut out of your life entirely. Trimpey talks about reintroducing the addict to the morality of using their substance of choice. He points to the distortion of morality the 12 step treatment programs, which says that drug/alcohol addiction is NOT a moral issue, but rather asserts it is a "chronic, mysterious, progressive disease." Trimpey accurately points out there's no real evidence for this disease, and that it's nothing more than an immoral choice—immoral because if the addict knows that even one use might cause them to get behind the wheel of a car and maim or mutilate another person, or to blow up the family finances, etc., then that first drink/use is nothing BUT an immoral choice.

I thoroughly agree with his assessment of the black and white addictions on this front. However, when it comes to food, the moral issue is MUCH less relevant. People simply don't get into bar fights and/or crash their cars after eating a box of donuts. What they do instead is go home and watch TV on the couch, feeling uncomfortably bloated, sleepy, and self-loathing. Yes, one could make an argument that it's immoral to slowly kill yourself with food, thereby leaving your family and other loved ones without your presence (and possibly your financial support depending upon your situation) to see them through. But that's a fairly weak argument because virtually everyone in our society seems to have tacitly agreed to slowly kill ourselves with food. Almost nobody maximizes their lifespan by eating as healthy as they possibly can. We ALL make serious trade-offs for personal pleasure with food. Where a behavior is ubiqui-

111

tous, the impact of denouncing it is minimal, so I quickly realized the moral argument wasn't going to work.

What DID work was the idea of committing with perfection but forgiving yourself with dignity. Practically speaking this means clearly defining your bullseye with rules (above), then committing to aim at that target with the totality of your being. An Olympic archer sees the arrow going into the target BEFORE they release the arrow. They don't allow themselves to be distracted by "maybe I'll hit it and maybe I won't" thoughts. They make all necessary adjustments and they OWN the goal before taking action. On the other hand, if they miss the bullseye, they allow themselves to feel the pain, analyze what might've gone wrong, make adjustments, and commit once again with perfection. What they do NOT do is engage in excessive self-castigation and/or allow themselves to get STUCK in the guilt or shame. They allow the pain of the mistake to get their attention for a moment, otherwise they couldn't fix the problem. But after they've made adjustments, they let it go. It's very much like the pain of having touched a hot stove. You WANT that pain – without it you won't be able to avoid the stove in the future. But you also don't want to say "Oh my God I'm such a pathetic hot stove toucher. I might as well just put my whole hand on the stove and leave it there!"

Commit with perfection and forgive yourself with dignity. That's the required mindset to overcome overeating.

➤ **COMPLEX FOOD RULES**: Another area in which I had to diverge from Jack Trimpey's plan for Rational Recovery was in the definition of "using" or "food abuse." With a lot of experimentation, I found it necessary to create a complex, but exquisitely clear set of rules for myself to define exactly what healthy vs. unhealthy food and food behavior was. Moreover, I found that if I left ANY ambiguity in these rules my Pig would take advantage and barrel right on through. I therefore ruthlessly pursued Food Rule revisions until I had a Food Plan the Pig couldn't assail.

➤ **AUTONOMOUS RULES**: I knew from my experience as a psychologist that people's relationship with food was very mixed up with their sense of independence and autonomy. Many of us were simply not fed in the right way, at the right times, and/or with the right foods despite our parents' insistence and best intentions. In short, we may have been *forced* to eat things which were not really in our best interest. I certainly knew I didn't want anyone telling ME what to eat. I therefore decided I would create my OWN rules, and that when and if I decided to work with clients, I would furiously avoid any attempt by their Pig to get me to tell them what to eat. I believed it would be essential that people created their own Food Plan. *(This is also a divergence from Rational Recovery. Trimpey did write a book on overcoming overeating, but my perception is that he missed the mark here with too much of an external emphasis on what "correct eating" was. I'm guessing the reason for this is the extraordinary amount of work he's done with alcohol and drugs where the external definition of use is crystal clear, as are its moral implications.)* If you listen to any of my demonstration sessions in this context (https://www.neverbingeagain.com/TheBlog/recorded-sessions/all-my-audios-all-in-one-place-updated/) you will see how passionate I am about helping people come to their OWN definition of healthy eating. I find if I make even the smallest mistake on this front, I'm then unable to really help the client.

There are two last things I'd like to say about the discovery of Never Binge Again which might be helpful to you, and which I haven't said elsewhere. The first one concerns the actual process by which one gets back on track after their Pig makes them feel like they've "lost it." The other concerns the input I had from other books and teaching sources that made the discovery of several of the divergences possible.

Getting Back on Track After You've "Lost It"

Ideally, if you're happy with your Food Plan (collective set of Food Rules), and assuming it's nutritionally and calorically sufficient, then the thing to do whenever you fall off by even a little bit is to get right back on. But sometimes people fall far off their Food Plan and keep repeating the mistake for days, weeks, or even months on end.

That happened to me in the very beginning. You can take comfort in the fact that if you keep going with Never Binge Again you CAN eliminate these periods entirely. Nevertheless, it might be helpful for you to understand there is an effective alternative to immediately attempting to reinstitute your entire Food Plan

The answer is usually to start with ONE simple, much less restrictive rule and work your way back to where you want to be with your Food Plan as a whole.

It was my literal experience with learning how to juggle which provided this insight. See, when I was an adolescent with a lot of time on my hands, I set out to learn how to juggle five balls at once. If you don't know anything about juggling, let me just repeat what I read in the book Juggling for the Complete Klutz: "On a scale of 1 to 10, learning how to juggle three balls is about a 6, learning how to juggle 4 balls is about an 11, and learning how to juggle five balls is a 37."

In other words, you were going to make a LOT of mistakes along the way. To give you a sense of how many, just know I got sore from bending down so much to pick up the balls. But eventually I got it, and I was exceptionally proud! Except every once in a while, it seemed like a mysterious thing had happened and I suddenly couldn't do it anymore, no matter how hard I tried. In fact, the harder I tried, the worse the problem became...

Until I decided to go back to juggling ONE ball and just observed the pattern. See, juggling is just a series of individual throws. When you learn how to juggle, you first practice throwing one ball up in a perfect arc and catching it. And you have to be able to precisely identify the moment in time when the ball stops going up and starts coming down, because that's when you have to throw the NEXT ball in a perfect arc.

So I had to go back to working with just ONE ball for a while, then edge back up to 2, then 3, then 4, then 5 again. **It finally "stuck" but I had to be really kind to myself while I was working on it. I couldn't insist on being where I really wanted to be right after the mistake. I had to let it slowly rebuild.**

Therefore, in the very beginning when I first started experimenting with a Never Binge Again Food Plan and I would "lose" it for a protracted period of time, I decided I had to "work my way back to five balls" (the comprehensive Food Plan) by reverting to following just ONE rule... and THAT did the trick.

For me that rule was almost always "I Will Never Eat Chocolate Again" because chocolate was the match that always seemed to light the binging fire. But for my clients it's always something different. **The question I ask them is "What is the simplest, easiest rule you could follow which might make the biggest difference?"**

If you're REALLY struggling to get back to your Food Plan as a whole, you may wish to ask yourself this question and forget the whole plan... just follow that ONE rule for a little bit until you regain your confidence.
I hope that helps.

Discovering the Divergences

I knew Jack Trimpey's thoughts on addiction had to be a big part of the answer for me, but I also knew there were problems associated with applying it to food. I was therefore relentless in continually trying variations until things came together. They finally DID come together for me because I spent a lot of time hiking listening to audio books entirely OUSIDE the realm of addiction!

In my 40s I lived in Southern New Hampshire just north of the border on route 93. And every week for at least one full day I would get in the car and drive about two hours north of that to the White Mountains for a hike...

This was one of the healthiest routines I ever integrated into my life. I'd make a few business calls while driving up and answer a few emails whenever I stopped to pee. But mostly I'd be listening to audio books the whole way up and back. I'd also be listening while I hiked in the woods. Philosophy, science, business, fiction. Everything. I loved the break from problem solving to just immerse myself in learning. I was a big fan of The Teaching Company, which recorded entire courses from college professors.

I found when I did this regularly that I never knew when something would later strike me as relevant for solving my business and personal problems. And there were two things which had a major impact...

The first one came from studying Einstein's General and Special Relativity. Without getting too technical, Einstein figured out that time and space were not the same for all observers. While they appeared to be fixed and constant, the speed at which the observer traveled made a difference. Not so much at the speeds we are accustomed to in our human existence, but as you approach any appreciable fraction of the speed of light things start to change. They also change in a strong gravitational field. *(These are proven facts now, not just theory. For example, if our GPS and satellite systems didn't account for them, they'd be off the mark.)*

What utterly fascinated me about this was the idea that you

could know something in one context and be absolutely SURE of it, while that thing could be utterly untrue in a different context. Shortly thereafter I read Atlas Shrugged by Ayn Rand and listened to several audio discussions of this material. One of the experts casually quipped that Rand had said "ALL knowledge is contextual!"

And that's when it all came together. "Progress not perfection" had to be contextually bound. It was a terrific mindset to use after you'd made a mistake because it helped you to first take the mistake seriously, but then to let go of the excess guilt and shame which I (and many other authors) KNEW was a very serious problem which only led to more binging. And so, just like Einstein had dared to ask "what if time and space don't apply in the way we are all accustomed to when we change the context", I asked myself whether "Progress not perfection" might not apply when one was COMMITTING to the pursuit of a goal, but only when one was trying to RECOVER from an eating mistake.

I then listened to a variety of motivational tapes which described the mindset of superior athletes and business performers and the answer hit me. PERFECTION. These people were committing with perfection, and as a result they could focus all their energy on the goal. All the "what if's" disappeared from their mind as they were concentrating on their bullseye.

You could and should switch between the two mindsets depending on which context you were in, pursuing the goal vs. recovering from mistakes. Commit with perfection but forgive yourself with dignity. And that, my friends, is where the insight came from! For a more detailed description of HOW to utilize this insight please see chapter three of Never Binge Again *(www.NeverBingeAgain.com)*.

My study of Einstein and all the philosophy tapes I listened to while hiking also gave me a penchant for the value of thought experiments, which you can see weaved into Never Binge Again throughout.

CHAPTER 9: MY 50S – GOING THROUGH TRAUMA WITHOUT OVEREATING

The first few years in my 50s hit me very hard. My ex and I had overcome the debt entirely, but we had very much grown apart in the process of accomplishing it. I'd built a successful marketing business AND coach training business, but we seriously disagreed on how I should pursue each of them. We were conflicting more and more, and neither one of them was as fulfilling as they should've been for me.

I also ran into another serious physical problem which was probably a remnant of the car accident in my 30s. I started to develop sciatica from working at a standing desk, and the doctors were telling me that I really couldn't do that anymore. I eventually solved the problem, but since I could not sit down and work for more than twenty minutes at a time without developing migraines (*I still can't*), this was a BIG problem and I was panicked.

I think because I'd gone through such serious physical problems in my 30s, this upset my ex very much. We'd been growing more distant ever since the financial disaster in 2001-2003, but at this point she started acting erratically towards me. To be fair, she might perceive I did the same with her.

Regardless of cause, I was very unhappy, and I started losing faith in the marriage. A few years thereafter I'd also lost trust, and that's the death sentence for any marriage. It became clear we were not meant to be together forever.

Having completely ruined my health in my thirties by binging my way through extreme stress, I was determined that no matter what happened this time, I would not make myself fat and sick. I had the Never Binge Again principles firmly in place and I was going to stick with them no matter what.

I published the book as I was contemplating divorce in 2015. It started taking off about six months later.

But the divorce wasn't the end of the traumatic time for me. On January 1st, 2016 my dog Zachary died. I know some people may not see that as a major trauma, but remember, I never had children, and by that point most of my friends were spread out all over the world. Since my ex and I weren't very close for about a decade prior, I'd really relied on my connection with Zachary. I was probably closer to him than any other living soul (http://www.neverbingeagain.com/images/ZachOnMountainTop.jpg).

Worse yet, my Mom suddenly passed away in the fall of 2017. Mom had been a constantly cheerful, funny, and loving presence in my life for the few years preceding the divorce, and especially in the months immediately leading up to it. http://www.neverbingeagagin.com/images/MommaLovesBananas.jpg

Almost immediately after my Mom died, I met and fell deeply in love with a very special woman who literally popped just up in my life unannounced on Facebook. It was like she knew I was alone and suffering. Within a few months though, it became clear there were insurmountable conflicts in that relationship too, and our break-up absolutely destroyed me.

By the way, I was 100% SURE we weren't right for each other and could NOT be together despite these feelings, and this was perhaps the quintessential test for me of my mantra "FEELINGS AREN'T FACTS." See, I'd learned through the failure of my marriage that "love is not enough." You've got to have SO many other things in place to forge a lifelong romantic partnership, and nobody knew better than me what those things were given all the couples I'd worked with in my 30s. It wasn't that I didn't love her anymore, or that I doubted her love for me... it's that we were factually incompatible, and I wouldn't allow myself to make another big mistake. Feelings aren't facts. *(I succumbed and tried again for about a week later on anyway, and re-experienced the trauma at a lower level. I think it was a way we both had of ending things more peacefully and, finally, permanently letting go.)*

I also had to slowly close down the coach training business after trying unsuccessfully to transfer it to my ex-wife without conflict. I'd become very attached to many of the students. It was awful.

And I moved across the country on my own, jettisoning virtually ALL my possessions. TWICE! *(Once to Portland, Oregon, and the second time to Ft. Lauderdale, Florida.)*

Throughout this entire time, however, I NEVER "lost it" with my eating. I had Never Binge Again to protect me, and in many ways, this was trial by fire for the new method. I managed to navigate all the traumatic changes with grace and dignity BECAUSE I wasn't constantly sacrificing my energy and presence to Pig Slop.

You may wish to remind yourself of my experience when you're feeling tempted to binge due to "stress" or difficult life circumstances. You don't need Pig Slop for "comfort", you need your wits about you—and presence of mind—so you can find solutions to your problems!

No matter what is happening in your life you do NOT have to binge. No matter what, no matter what, no matter what! If you have six problems and then you binge, you'll have seven prob-

lems!

PS – As I was finishing this book I got news that I *might* have a mild form of Parkinson's disease. If I have six problems and I overeat, I'll have seven problems. *(This one is actually not a big problem because if the diagnosis is made, my life will actually get better due to the available treatment. But the news temporarily terrified me until I learned more, so the mantra was helpful indeed!)*

There's No Chlorophyll in Bacon – The Journey to My Current Dietary Philosophy

My long, long journey away from food addiction brought me to what most people would characterize as a very extreme diet, though now, from my perspective, *what everyone else does is extreme and what I do is normal!* Doug Graham taught me that when people try to dismiss me as a "health nut" I should explain to them this is untrue... I am a "health enthusiast!" And it was only when I became willing to fully embrace this, rather than accepting the denigrating labels people were putting on me, that I was able to embrace a diet which so thoroughly supported my nutritional and caloric needs that the cravings diminished dramatically.

To illustrate how important it is to get nutrition right for your body, I often tell my clients "There are some rules you can't make. For example, you can't say 'I will never pee again!' because your body will show you otherwise. Similarly, you can't restrict your genuine nutritional or caloric needs for too long or your survival instincts will force you to be less discriminating about food... all your rules be damned!

Before I explain where I landed though in terms of my own dietary philosophy, I'd like to say three things:

> ➢ I'd venture to say 70% of the variance in car injuries

might be explained by safe driving or the lack thereof, and only 30% by the safety of the actual vehicle you drive. So, you COULD obsess about the absolute safest car to drive and put all your time, energy, and money into acquiring it —OR—you could focus on driving safely. Of course, it's important to do both, but on balance I think it's much better to allocate your resources to DRIVING SAFELY.

Similarly, it's much more important, in my estimation, to stop binge eating and overeating than to eat the exact right healthy diet.

Moreover, as discussed previously, binge eaters in particular have serious problems with being told what to do. It's like we have a big rebellious monster inside us. For this reason, I find it critical to respect people's autonomy when it comes to selecting a diet. It's no secret I'm not personally a fan of ketogenic and/or low-carb diets myself... but fully HALF my clients aggressively pursue this dietary style. I support them if they so desire, because in my estimation it's about four million times better than binge eating! And who knows, maybe they're onto something I don't really understand or can't see through my scientific eyes. That said, let me just note here that I have seen less long-term success on the ultra-low-carbohydrate versions of the ketogenic diet than those which are more moderate.

➢ Although I've studied nutrition and the human diet more so than most, and I DO believe in the concept of a species specific diet *(I think there is ONE truth regarding what each and every particular species on the planet is most optimally designed to eat – including humans)* I have not taken it to the level where I'd be able to argue it in a professional debate, nor do I wish to. Professionally, I'm a coach, psychologist, marketer, businessperson, and a modestly handsome, compassionate, and funny guy... NOT a dietitian and/or medical doctor.

Notwithstanding my formal position on helping each person to decide their personal Food Plan for themselves, I have had a very distinct journey, and each step along the way represented a significant improvement in my personal progress. In the event any of these steps might help you, I'd like you to know!

Please note that I NEVER thought binging on chocolate, pizza, and Pop-Tarts was healthy. Even in my worst, heaviest, most binge-laden years I always had a healthy bullseye towards which I aimed. I just wasn't able to come very close to that bullseye because I didn't know how to keep my Pig in the Cage until my early to mid-40s.

So what follows is the evolution of my thinking about the ideal diet over the many years I struggled.

When I was in high school, my mother was diagnosed with fibroid tumors in her uterus, as well as cysts in her ovaries. She was advised to have a hysterectomy but was absolutely terrified of the operation. So, she took the advice of an acupuncturist who suggested she skip surgery and remove all animal products from her diet for a year...

And it worked! The fibroids receded and the cysts were gone.

Moreover, during those years the family was a lot healthier. There were always salads and fruit in the house. Of course, all the junk food was still there too, so it was NOT a whole-foods, plant-based diet...but we all had a LOT more energy. And Mom felt like it was a miracle – she beat the system.

Two years later Mom was back to eating the way she always had. She did live to 77 years old, but suffered tremendously through three rounds of ovarian cancer, two heart attacks, and a stroke. *(She also fell down the stairs three times and broke all sorts of things.)*

I always wished Mom had stayed on the no-animal-products diet, so I moved my bullseye progressively more towards that philosophy in college. However, as you already know by now, I REALLY didn't have the impulse control to maintain that, so I was constantly eating eggs, cheese, pizza, and fish too. Every day.

Towards the end of college, I read a book called Fit for Life by Harvey and Marilyn Diamond. They had much to say about when you ate what, and in what combination, but there was a heavy emphasis on fruit and vegetables. My whole family read it and started trying to implement it again. It still included a lot of animal products, but it was a step in the right direction as far as I was concerned. This book also gave me permission to eat a lot of fruit in the morning, which became an integral part of my final solution.

But it wasn't until I reached graduate school and was a little more separate from the family that I could get back to the no-animal products diet again myself. I managed to do this success-fully for a year, although I affectionately call this year my "junk food vegan" epoch. While I didn't eat animal foods, I largely lived on pasta, French fries, cereal, and sugary snacks. I was by no means healthy at this time, and in many ways my Pig devel-oped even stronger. It's very easy to use a dietary philosophy to justify feeding your Pig!

It was also in my twenties that my Pig really came into full bloom and I started gaining weight in earnest. I continued with the no-animal-products ideal throughout my twenties, though I cheated so often you'd never know it from the outside.

In my early thirties, a good friend of mine got involved at a rather high level with the Atkins company. Another friend of mine became a nutritional counselor and was advising people to eat a very low carbohydrate diet. And this is also when my ex-wife adopted this philosophy, which I believe she remains on to this day.

For a few years I thought this was the answer, and I kept aiming at a diet filled with chicken, salmon, and sardines...but I never could stick for very long. When I fell off, I fell HARD, and my Pig came out big time.

By my mid-thirties I'd accepted that my ex and I were not going to eat the same, and I revised my bullseye to be largely whole foods, but I included a lot of fish, and some chicken. I'd read a book called "The Chilton Diet" which focused on the inflammatory impact of arachidonic acid in particular types of meat, so I reasoned if I ate low-arachidonic index foods along with avoiding processed stuff, I'd be fine. This might've worked, at least a lot better than what I'd been doing, but of course I was still Pig obsessed and couldn't stick with it for very long at any given time.

I was in and out of Overeaters Anonymous during these years too, and that's where I learned to measure my food. I was thin for a stretch while in OA, but the moment I made a mistake they told me that I'd fallen into some abyss and had to pray for my higher power to pull me out of it. My Pig loved that – the perfect excuse to binge more, which I did.

I finished my thirties with the years of financial disaster, undiagnosed Lyme disease, and chronic migraines. During this period, I'd given up almost entirely on eating healthy. I went through an "all bets are off" phase where I just didn't care and let my Pig run wild. This made me feel worse than awful, and as covered many times before in this book, was completely unnecessary.

NEVER ALLOW A PERIOD IN YOUR LIFE WITH NO FOOD BULLSEYE! NEVER ALLOW CHAOS TO REIGN NO MATTER WHAT YOUR PIG SAYS!

That's like trying to live in a society with no rules and no laws. Anarchy is the only result, and nothing good ever comes from that. ANY bullseye is better than allowing chaos to reign. You must always know what you believe is healthy vs. unhealthy eating. In the absence of this your Pig will grow much stronger.

It wasn't until my early 40s that I discovered the Never Binge Again method and began to slowly recover my weight, my health, and my sanity. In terms of the food bullseye, there were three distinct phases...

In phase one, which lasted about two years and corresponded to my having found Dr. Fuhrman's "Eat to Live" book *(and the rest of his work)*, I continued to believe whole foods were the answer. But I cut back dramatically on animal products. I really respected Dr. Fuhrman's emphasis on scientific evidence.

As a very important aside, the public doesn't really understand the difference between junk science and real science, which makes it possible for marketers and news seekers to use junk science to dominate the airwaves. Real science though, is replicable, controlled, accurately reported, and not funded by industry with an agenda. Junk science often consists of one or two shoddily conducted and reported studies, which the public eats up with a vengeance, and which marketers use with abandon. This is the main reason for so much confusion about diet in the population, I believe. Howie Jacobson, Ph.D., my frequent podcast compadre, good friend, and author of "Sick to Fit" says "The public just eats up 'good news about their bad habits' and its killing them!"

Anyway, because Never Binge Again was beginning to be very effective for me, I lived fairly close to my food bullseye for the first time in my life and it felt GREAT!

There's an important concept in psychology called "The Ego Ideal" and it's distinct from your actual ego. It recognizes that there's always an ideal towards which the ego strives but can never quite fully achieve. There is therefore always some distance between ego and ego ideal. The less distance, the better the individual's self-esteem, the more distance, the worse.

For this reason, I started to feel dramatically better about myself in my early 40s. I was closing the gap! *(It's worth noting you can also close the gap by lowering your ego ideal – and this is often part of the process of recovery for binge eaters)*

Early into phase one I came down to about 220 pounds and stabilized there. I wasn't doing any type of heavy weight lifting or muscle building, so this was still a little heavy for me, but quite an accomplishment compared to where I came from *(about 280 at my max)*. I'd been lighter during my years in Overeaters Anonymous, but it wasn't sustainable.

In phase two I cut out animal products completely. This corresponded to when Dr. Furhman revised his recommendation for the percentage of calories from animal products in the diet from 10% to 5%. I'm guessing it began when I was about 45 years old and lasted until I was 50. Cutting out animal products entirely had a dramatic impact on my health. Suddenly, after struggling with psoriasis for twenty years, I had NONE. The chief dermatologist at a major teaching hospital in NYC said he wasn't sure he could still make a rosacea diagnosis on me because my symptoms vanished entirely too. And I just barely struggled with eczema anymore.

Obviously there was some sort of inflammatory process I managed to arrest by giving up meat, dairy, fish, and eggs...and because Never Binge Again was working, I could keep to the diet very closely. It was a miracle, and I benefited it SO many ways. Dr. Furhman also has a specific set of recommendations for which plant foods to eat in order to increase your immunity, and I found that after a few months of following it I got sick about half as often, the symptoms were half as intense, and lasted half as long. It was a real bump in my quality of life on so very many levels!

When people beg me to suggest I diet, I suggest they read Eat to Live and consider doing the no-animal-products, gluten-free version of it. In my experience, when people can adopt this bulls eye, it produces a high level of satisfaction, a minimum of confusion, and is very sustainable.

Now, I DID move on from Dr. Furhman's diet to a food bullseye which might be considered a subset of it, which I consider to be even healthier, and which has done even more for me. Before I explain that, however, I want you to know that it is exceptionally rare that it took me several years to make it work, and the vast majority of my clients who try do so for only a month or two and then, well, run away screaming. I STILL believe it's the healthiest way for humans to eat, and I DO STRONGLY SUGGEST YOU READ THE BOOK *("The 80-10-10 Diet"*, but mostly just so you know where your FUTURE bullseye may lie. Because such a small percentage of my clients succeed on this diet in the short run, because overcoming binge eating is the MOST important dietary adjustment you can make in the short run, and because Dr. Fuhrman's diet is much easier to sustain in the short run, I usually recommend that people start there. Remember, it took ME several years on a just slightly modified Eat to Live bullseye before I was ready to move to this next level.

In any case, what I presently consider to be the ultimate in human nutrition is the 80-10-10 philosophy. What it basically says is "Eat a LOT of raw, organic fruit and leafy greens, a LITTLE raw nuts and seeds, and absolutely nothing else." The key being in the A LOT part, which is a lot harder than it sounds. It takes some getting used to physically. It takes a lot of planning, shopping, and preparation. It requires you to learn new negotiation skills for fruit purchasing AND changes to where and how you shop unless you want to take out a second mortgage, and if you don't have enough volume it not only won't work, you'll be even more motivated to binge because your body will be calorically and/or nutritionally deprived. And you must watch for nutritional deficiencies and supplement appropriately because certain nutrients are no longer present in the way they were before agriculture.

But if you DO pull it off, you'll feel amazing. Superhuman, really

—although I believe this is exactly how humans were designed to feel before all the processing and cooking began.

I feel so strongly about this bullseye that the small tattoo on my right arm says "raw vegan." There are actually several different types of raw veganism, and the 80-10-10 variety is the low-fat type because it points to science that says fat functions as an insulator in the blood which makes it very difficult for sugar to exit the bloodstream. This is what, Doug Graham argues, causes the sugar metabolic problems like diabetes, and he goes so far as to run retreats for diabetics, showing them how their A1C and other metrics come measurably down over the course of just a few days on this diet. Evaluate this for yourself with your doctor please, but I personally was very impressed.

Despite my thorough commitment to this bullseye, I periodically change my Food Plan to allow cooked whole grains and beans when I'm going through a difficult period without enough time to do the work to maintain a 100% raw vegan diet. As the years go by, these periods are less and less frequent, because every time I DO change the plan, I feel much worse than I do when I'm on it.

I also have a medical condition called a benign tremor which motivates me to avoid cooked food. There are some chemicals formed when food is cooked called heterocyclic amines which have been shown to aggravate the tremor in some people, and I'm apparently one of them. Still, there are time when life calls for some compromises and I make adjustments.

You'll find, over the years, as you work the Never Binge Again methodology, that you go through periods of "installing" new Food Rules and striving for progressively healthier ways of eating and being, whatever this means to you. There will always be some distance between your ideal bullseye and the way you are actually able to eat. That's OK, as long as you keep striving, and continue to commit with perfection yet forgive yourself with dignity for mistakes. You NEVER reach a state of

perfection, but you ALWAYS strive for it.

Keep at it, and maybe one day you too will be eaten by a shark, and that would be bad-ass, wouldn't it?

CHAPTER 10: THE FINAL WORD

ARE YOU DONE HARMING YOURSELF WITH FOOD?

There's a dietary leader who said two things which had a very profound impact on me. One was "You should never have to recover from a meal", and the other was "I am DONE harming myself with food!"

Both of those mantras stuck with me. I can sometimes still hear them in his voice.

I don't know about you, but I am DONE harming myself with food. I spent WAY too much time passing things through my body that didn't belong there. Trying to digest Slop that was obviously meant more for Pigs than my human self. Spending hours hating myself, sweating and bloated on the coach.

Are you DONE?

If so, get mad and stay mad...

Be mad at the Big Food industry for continuing to manufacture ever more sophisticated food-like-substances which fool us into thinking we need THEM to survive, instead of what nature has to offer...

Be mad at the Big Advertising industry, which uses ever more sophisticated ways to convince us that we can't live without this junk...

And be mad at the 12 Step syndicate, which has flooded the

culture with the "addiction is a disease" and "you are powerless in the face of these temptations" nonsense. Really, it's nothing more than "the devil made me do it" prairee poop packaged up in a contagious religious framework.

But most of all, get angry at your Pig for lying to you all these years... for telling you half-truths and thinly disguised arguments to convince you to suffer with ever more episodes of "one last time." Really, how many last suppers are you going to feed it!!?

ARE YOU DONE HARMING YOURSELF WITH FOOD!!??

I know I am. Because in the absence of that declaration my life would be only a fraction of what it is and/or could be. I have barely 1/20th the potential with Slop inside me than without.

So take a breath and repeat after me: "Yes Glenn, I AM done harming myself with food, forevermore! My last bite of Pig Slop is behind me, whether that's 5 seconds, 5 minutes, 5 days, or 5 years ago. I AM DONE"

Need help? Click below now!

www.FixYourFoodProblem.com

APPENDIX A – MY ANCESTORS

I don't know that much about my ancestors as my parents and grandparents didn't seem to want to talk about them. I think there was good reason for that as the few stories they told highlighted some very painful and traumatic events.

I did, however, recently interview and record several hours with each of my parents to document as much as I could while the memories were still fresh. Here's what I know, at least the important stuff.

My Mom's Side

My mother's father "Pa Mike" was abandoned to an orphanage when my great-grandmother "Lena" immigrated from Russia in approximately 1914, just before World War I. Apparently, his father, my great grandfather, owned a very successful candy store in Moscow. Is his profession a big surprise given my history?

Anyway, he was doing very well financially when he was suddenly killed in a horse carriage accident. Between this event and what was happening politically in the country, great-grandma Lena decided it would be best to come to the United States. Unfortunately, she didn't have enough money to take care of two children when she got here, so she put my grandfather in an orphanage in Chicago, choosing to keep his brother only.

The brother (my great-uncle) became a very successful attorney and raised a large family, of whom I know little to nothing about. My grandfather, on the other hand, led a very difficult life and became a criminal. He eventually got caught for stock fraud and spent a few years in prison right around the time I was in my mother's womb.

This devastated Mom and her resulting depression was, in part, responsible for difficulty feeding me correctly. I've also heard stories from my Mom's brother Steve about visiting my grand-father in prison. "It's a horrible, horrible place Glenn – always stay on the right side of the law – crime isn't worth it" he said.

Interestingly I didn't know any of this story until I was at least 19 years old but had always felt an irrational fear of being falsely accused and sent to prison. The fear eased after I learned about this, but to this day I'm a "goodie goodie" about complying with the law, more so than most people I know. I drive the speed limit, pay my taxes, and don't spit on the sidewalk. There are worse fates in life.

Nine months after I was born, however, Pa Mike was released from prison and turned over a new leaf. He bought and ran a very small diner and was doing modestly well. He poured a lot of his attention, and what love he still had in his heart into ME. In fact, because my Dad was working a lot, Pa Mike spent more time with me in my early childhood than my father did.

Pa Mike is also largely responsible for my sense of humor. Well, also my mother's infectious laugh. But Pa Mike taught things in really fun ways. For example, when he wanted to teach me about electronic circuitry, he went out and got a few magnetic switches. Then one day when nobody else was home we wired them to the toilet and connected them to a tape recorder/player. About ten seconds after anyone opened the toilet seat to sit down it would say "Oh no! Don't do it! Please! There's some-one down here!!"

When I'd have some friends from school sleep over Pa Mike

would wake us up at 2 am saying "time for pizza kids!" And he was fond of taking his teeth out and holding them in his hands at the dinner table when any of my friends weren't looking. As soon as they turned towards them, he'd make a chomp-chomp motion at them with his teeth.

But Pa Mike also taught me how to exercise, play baseball, build a fire, and use a computer at a very early age. *(Remember, I grew up in the 60s and 70s so access to computers was very scarce).* And he was always giving me things. Toys, games, books, learning tools... and food! Pa Mike loved cooking more than anything else. My favorite wasn't anything fancy though – he made "noodles and cheese" which was just bowtie pasta with cottage cheese on top. I couldn't get enough.

My mother's mother "Ma Pearl" was born here but her mother "Lena" was from Poland. The most famous story about Lena was about her immigration. Immediately after stepping off the boat at Ellis Island in New York City, Lena was diagnosed with Smallpox. The authorities placed a small mark to indicate this on her arm and directed her to the medical line. Fearing she'd be sent back home, she wiped off the mark and snuck back into the main line, successfully immigrating but perhaps spreading the disease. Lena's last name was "Kahan" which denoted a line of famous Rabbi's in Poland, but the authorities changed it to Cohen, which she kept until marrying.

I don't know my great-grandfather's name (Lena's husband) on my mother's side, but I do know he died just after my mother was born. Not long after this Lena developed schizophrenia, was often catatonic, and refused to clean her room and/or use the bathroom. However, she had a real soft spot for my mother and would often hold, cuddle, and shelter my Mom from my grandmother Pearl when Pearl would become abusive towards my mother. Lena was hospitalized several times in my mother's childhood, and eventually died when she stopped taking her diabetes medication.

I know very little about my Mom's side of the family before 1900.

My Dad's Side

The most significant event in my father's history was that his father ("George") died of a kidney disease when dad was just four years old. George was a high school gym teacher, loved by all, and the family, particularly his mother, was devastated. George was also an extremely handsome man. I like to think I got at least a little of his looks. In the Jewish tradition you name your first-born son using the first initial of the name of an ancestor you want to honor. I'm named "Glenn" after grandpa George, whom I never met.

My grandmother Esther "Ma Esta" became very depressed after George died. Thankfully for my dad though, there was a large extended family nearby, and they moved in with my great grandfather "Pop", my grandmother "Dora", their children, and several of Grandma Esta's brothers and sisters. Esther was one of seven children.

Dad was apparently surrounded by these people night and day and his memories of them appear to be some of the fondest in his life. I've met several of my dad's 7 aunts and uncles once or twice, and they did indeed light up when they saw him. On dad's 65th birthday my ex-wife arranged a surprise party and flew as many of them in as she could. I learned a few very interesting things that day, including the fact that my great-great grand-father was a mobster in Hungary in the late 1800s who used to ride around town on a bull. I also learned one of Dad's uncles was a general in the army during WW2 who got busted down to Lt. Colonel because he allowed the Japanese to land on the Aleutian Islands in USA territory. But mostly, I learned that my dad was loved and adored by these people, and that was very settling and inspiring to see.

We didn't have very much contact with Dad's side of the family though, because Dad wasn't very close with his mother. She'd become very critical of him as part of her depression in mourning, and dad could never really bridge the gap. I saw Grandma Esther maybe a half dozen times in my entire life. At about 24 years old, shortly after I got married, I drove by myself to visit her. Without thinking, I took her to see an R-rated movie, and I learned that's NOT something you want to do with your grandma! *(I had to sit and squirm during the sex scenes.)* When Ma Esta was dying in my mid-30s I went to her apartment again to visit and was surprised to see she had pictures of my sister and I plastered all around. It's sad, really – I would've liked to have known her better.

When Dad was about 9 years old Esther remarried a man named Jack Livingston, which is where my name comes from. Most people are surprised to know I'm Jewish, and that the original family name was "Sandleman" ... but Esther took Jack's name and Jack adopted my father.

Dad was very unhappy about the new marriage, however, because although Jack was wealthy, Dad and his mom had to move out of the Brooklyn, NY home where he was loved and adored by all, into a situation with an older step brother and sister who weren't very happy to have him around. Dad had some trouble adjusting in school, and basically became depressed himself. He didn't have great grades and had to work hard to get into college.

What Dad did have going for him, however, was extreme intelligence, and a good heart. When he decided he might like to be a psychologist and pursued that whole hog, he catapulted through, wound up getting his Ph.D. from Columbia University, and built a successful practice in relatively short order when the time came. This made him and Mom the first upwardly mobile people in a family of Jewish Immigrants...

And set the template for literally more than a dozen other family members to enter psychology as a business.

What You Can Learn from Your Ancestors

I once attended a workshop entitled "It didn't start with you", the gist of which was that you should honor your ancestors' lifetime of suffering by thriving, not by suffering more. It was very moving and changed my perspective on the whole thing. I recorded a podcast about it which you can listen to here... the odds are it will alter your perspective too.

APPENDIX B – RANDOM THINGS ABOUT ME YOU MIGHT FIND HELPFUL AND/OR ENTERTAINING

A few things about me personally that didn't fit anywhere else.

My Favorite Thing I Ever Said

My favorite thing I ever said is **"The name of the game is staying in the game until you win the game!"** It applies to just about everything, but overeating in particular.

See, our Inner Pigs are very fond of berating us and making us feel pathetic whenever we make a mistake. But the truth is, research proves people who finally discover their own solution to stop overeating and reach their ideal weight (or close to it) for good are those who make the most attempts...

Put simply, winners keep getting up no matter how many times they fall down. The name of the game is staying IN the game until you win the game!

So if Never Binge Again "failed" you, or perhaps worked really well out of the gate but then stopped when something out of the ordinary came up *(e.g. a trip, pressure at work, a challenging time with your family, or perhaps it just got cold and you couldn't exercise anymore)*...

which then led to a loosening of your food rules OR your compliance with them...

Which led to gaining back some or all of the weight you lost *(perhaps more)*...

Then there's something really important you need to know. This happens to MOST people who use Never Binge Again, including those who eventually become permanently successful. It's a very normal course. Their Pig makes a much bigger deal out of it than it is and says things like "This isn't working, just like every other diet we've tried before, it's failed, which means YOU are a failure and should just give up and become a happy fat person already!"

Does that sound familiar? If so, your Pig has put you back in the Matrix where you live in a simulated reality where the Pig has convinced you NOTHING can work so you might as well just binge your face off.

But look, people who succeed with NBA long term understand that slip-ups and set-backs are part of the game...even though they must commit to aiming at the bullseye with perfect each time anew. What successful people also understand is that perhaps the most important part of the NBA system is recovering as quickly as possible... and not letting the Pig use it's "failure, shame and guilt" bit on you.

Cultivate a success identity no matter what happens. "Commit with perfection but forgive yourself with dignity." If you play THAT game long enough, and recover as many times as necessary, the rules become a part of who you are, and you can permanently defeat the Pig in the long run.

It's like an archer... if you keep getting up and aiming at the bullseye anew your aim MUST get better, because human beings are set up as neurological learning machines. The reason people get worse is they let all these crazy voices extend the errors and prevent their renewed attempts.

"Fall down seven times, get up eight" – Japanese Proverb.

The name of the game is staying in the game until you win the game!

Six Ideas That Mean the World to Me

1. "A life of discipline is better than a life of regret." - Jim Rohn. Freedom sits on top of discipline. If it weren't for the discipline of the engineers who built your car, the wheels wouldn't turn 30 degrees to the right when you turned the steering wheel precisely that amount, the car wouldn't move faster when you hit the gas and slower when you hit the brakes. You wouldn't have the freedom to drive where you wanted, when you wanted, and your world would be exponentially smaller. Freedom REQUIRES discipline - so don't shun discipline, embrace it! What new discipline could you add to enhance your life today?

2. The fundamental choice in life is whether to get well or get even. Most people give lip service to the idea that they've chosen a life of forgiveness, gratefulness, and love... but if you sit where I have with thousands of clients who tell you the intimate details of their lives, you'll see there's a big difference between saying you're living for love and actually doing it. It's only human to be tempted to get even. We have ALL suffered at the hands of others. Even when the other didn't intend to do harm - stupidity is unfortunately rampant in human relations. So, I don't fault people for having the feelings. It requires strength and determination to choose to get well instead every day. Which will you choose?

3. "You can have anything you want but you can't have everything you want." - Peter McWilliams. It's true - most people dramatically underestimate the power of one person on an organized and determined mission to effect virtually any change they want to... provided they are persistent, resilient, and focused. And most people dramatically overestimate what they can accomplish in one year (so they give up), while dramatically underestimating what they can accomplish in five years. What one thing do YOU want?

4. Real love takes five to ten years. It's easy to say "I love you", but infinitely harder to show up consistently for another human being in the way they need most.

5. "Democracy is the worst form of government - except for all the others" - Winston Churchill. If communism worked, I'd support it. After all, it's about time we move away from tribalism and consider ourselves to be citizens of one world...but I'm nowhere near convinced it's possible to pull it off effectively. But we need serious restraints on capitalism to prevent greed and corruption from ruining what we've built.

6. "Support the walls people put up and they'll eventually start peaking around them." This is MY quote. It comes from the early days of my therapy practice when I tried all sorts of ways to blast through people's defenses so they could make "progress." Eventually I figured out people had reasons for putting up these walls. And they weren't going to come out from behind those walls until I made them feel safe enough *(and loved enough)* to do it. Getting there required that I adopt an attitude of GENTLE INTRIGUE until they had the courage to think new thoughts and risk new behaviors. Turns out, having an attitude of gentle intrigue with yourself isn't such a bad idea either!

Nine Life-Giving Insights from Glenn's Most Recent Years on the Planet:

1. Eat some fruit. Do some yoga. Breathe. It's not complicated.

2. A fundamental life choice we all face is whether to get well or get even. Most people SAY they've chosen to get well - but aligning your behavior with this choice is a real challenge, and most people unconsciously act in such a way as to get even. The get-even drive is very strong in humans. I know personally it requires a serious mental effort to overcome it.

3. Trust people to the extent they prove themselves trustworthy. Trust is something to earned, treasured, and protected in a relationship. Not something to be blindly given until you're proven wrong.

4. To program your mind for success it's necessary to ask "How Can I?" NOT "Why Can't I?" The questions we ask determine the evidence we collect about ourselves. The evidence we collect determines the identity we develop. The identity we develop determines the actions we take. And actions determine our success vs. failure. "How can I _____?"

5. We should NEVER have to recover from a meal. (*I got this from Doug Graham*)

6. You can't ever feel 100% secure because there's NO way to know everything that might happen. In this sense, security is always, to at least a certain extent, an illusion.

7. Commit with perfection but forgive yourself with dignity. Put every fiber of your being into pursuing your goal. If you miss the bullseye, don't castigate yourself - just analyze what went wrong, adjust, and pursue with a perfect commitment again.

8. Floss. For f---k's sake, floss!!

9. What you miss when you give up certain short-term gratifica-

tion genuinely pales in comparison to what you get by sticking with it.

The Voice of Contrarian Reason

In my 40s I focused largely on teaching marketing and building an ad agency. I used my research skills as a competitive advantage. Nothings more powerful than asking a market what it wants and then just giving it to them, especially when you break that market up into groups of like-minded people with similar desires. That was my #1 money making secret.

But there was something else, something VERY powerful, which I discovered during those years which shaped my thinking about how to present Never Binge Again to the public. Want to know what my #2 marketing secret is?

Digging deep for something I passionately believe is right in a market DESPITE what everyone else is doing and saying, then being the voice of contrarian reason... standing up and shouting it from the roof tops.

It's a habit I developed as a psychologist working with clinical patients. You see, when you're in the room with a patient, it's just you and them. And most psychological problems originate when people's inner sense of what's right was beaten out of them in one way, shape, or form. So your patient would count on you to have the courage to point it out. To take a stand against the crowd. To be the only one truly on their side until they have the strength to believe in their own convictions.

What I discovered when working with suicidal people was that you had to get them to feel that at least one person in the world thoroughly understood what they were going through. Because that's frequently all it took to give people the hope and courage to go on. As a side effect, it also happens to bond people to you for life. (*Seriously, I haven't formally solicited clinical psychology clients in 10 years, but I still get people calling in every year, some willing to drive 350 miles to come in for a single catch up session)*

We all live on hope and courage, don't we?

Now, of course, this isn't a lesson on treating suicidal patients it's a marketing tip *(and if you happen to treat, coach, or love someone who is suicidal, please get direct, professional supervision and assistance)* ...

But as I developed my marketing career, I discovered this has EVERYTHING to do with marketing.

Here's why.

We live in an insane world. People are cruel to one another wherever you look. Not purposefully cruel, but because *(in the absence of a seriously self-reflective and educated orientation)* human nature is greedy, lustful, self-centered, lazy, and aggressive, things just drift in that direction.

People's natural inclination is to exploit one another, and nowhere is this truer than in business.

In every market, vendors will take whatever they can from their consumers. And "marketing incest" coupled with a general lack of research usually ensures companies will copy from one another, leaving the consumer feeling like "this is normal".

But it's not.

In every market you thoroughly research you'll find there are always at least a few excruciatingly painful, unmet needs...

A consumer looking for a champion...

For someone to stand up against the crowd and say "the emperor has no clothes", "this is wrong and I'm not going to take it anymore", "why is no one talking about this", etc.

Being the voice of contrarian reason might look like this in different markets:

➢ MARKETING: "You can't market based on FAQs alone. Frequently Asked Questions are also Frequently Answered Questions... they only represent "price of entry" benefits (what every vendor needs to even be considered in the running)... you've got to sell "point of difference" benefits to get people to open up their wallets, answering the problems and questions the competition isn't! Why isn't anyone talking about this?

➢ GUINEA PIGS: The standard pet food and bedding materials recommended for your guinea pigs are cutting his little life in half! Why am I the only one saying anything?

➢ RABBITS: You absolutely CAN litter train your rabbit and get it to live 8 years+. Rabbits are better pets than cats, and it's about time someone said so!

➢ RADON: You CAN still get lung cancer from Radon UNDER your state's reporting threshold. It's an outrage! (Note: radon is an invisible, odorless, but radioactive and carcinogenic gas found in many locations)

➢ EMOTIONAL EATING: Stop dieting and start losing weight. Learn to enjoy eating the same delicious foods you love now without stress and without guilt.

➢ SUDOKU: You can solve EVERY sudoku puzzle, not just some, but every last one!

➢ WEIGHT LOSS: Guidelines don't work because they wear down your willpower with constant decision making. Hard and fast rules are much better. Overeating isn't a disease, it's a healthy appetite corrupted by industry. You shouldn't cultivate fear of your own impulse to eat, cultivate confidence instead.

See what I mean?

Now, how do you get to this in your market?

Intriguingly, you first have to find the courage in yourself. What is it that YOU personally believe despite everything that everyone seems to say all around you? Get out a journal and write until you figure that out. Because it's amazing how your eyes open up to your market once you've had the personal experience.

Personally, I believe everyone struggles with anxiety and depression to one degree or another. While there certainly does exist a more severe set of diagnostic categories *(for which medication, psychotherapy, etc. can help)*, the truth is we all like to categorize it as "mental illness" to protect ourselves from the truth.

And the truth is that in the world we live in, how could anyone really open their eyes and not feel at least a little anxious and depressed? It's normal and healthy to recognize this. And in my estimation if you want to be a strong marketer, it's essential.

Because staying out of touch with reality takes a lot of mental energy, and prevents you from seeing other people's true pain, their true motivations, and their true needs.

And that's what marketing is all about.

So... what do you think?

The voice of contrarian reason played very strongly in my head as I wrote Never Binge Again. I was keenly aware how badly mistreated consumers were being treated in our modern society by the Big Food Industry, Big Advertising, and Big Addiction Treatment. I was also immensely aware of how diametrically opposed the REAL solution was vs. what is still, to this day, purported to work.

Don't Stop When You're Tired – Stop When You're Done

DON'T STOP WHEN YOU'RE TIRED, STOP WHEN YOU'RE DONE!

I was listening to an audio book my partner recommended today on my long drive. One of the principles espoused was the above quote "don't stop when you're tired, stop when you're done"

I love that.

I know so many of you have fallen down repeatedly. Whether it's on a diet, a career path, a relationship effort. And I know you're TIRED of having to keep getting back up…

But did you know that people who eventually find a way to lose weight and keep it off have significantly more attempts behind them? That people who eventually DO find love had a multitude of failed attempts behind them? That most people with successful careers have had painful, nerve-wracking failures at every turn?

The name of the game really IS staying in the game until you win the game. Winners keep getting up until they win.

So, don't stop because you're tired. Stop when the job is done.

Food for thought on this fine Tuesday evening, which some people call Christmas.

All my love, people!

Stand for Something!

"IF YOU DON'T STAND FOR SOMETHING YOU WILL FALL FOR ANYTHING" - Alexander Hamilton

I've always loved this quote, and I think it summarizes the essence of what works in Never Binge Again…

148

See, if you walk around willy-nilly thinking you're just going to "eat healthy"... but you haven't taken the time to define EXACTLY what that means to you...

If you don't know what you do and don't consider to be part of your Food Plan...

If you're not crystal clear on what's healthy vs. unhealthy for you personally...

Then you make yourself infinitely vulnerable to the food industry's manipulations...

You can be talked into believing ANYTHING is good for you...

Or at least "not so bad" for you...

Things like: palm oil, shortening, white flour, white rice, high fructose corn syrup, aspartame, saccharin, sucralose sodium benzoate, potassium benzoate, benzene, butylated hydroxyanisole (BHA), sodium nitrate and sodium nitrites, blue, green, red, and yellow carcinogenic food dyes, MSG, hygrogenated and partially hydrogenated vegetable oils, sodium phosphate, interesterified fat, evaporated cane juice, brominated vegetable oil, hydrolized vegetable protein, modified food starch, caramel coloring, azodicarbonamide, propylene glycol, disodium inosinate, disodium guanylate, recombinant bovine growth hormone (rBGH), propyl gallate, sodium carboxymethyl cellulose, aluminum, bleached starch, tert butylhydroquinone...

EVEN FLAVORED CARDBOARD is permitted in some jurisdictions. (I'm NOT making this up!)

The solution is to stand for something. What kind of person do you want to be around food? What role will XYZ food and/or substance and/or food behavior play in your life?

Stand for something or you will fall for anything.

Be someone - it's just a better way to live.

If you don't have a plan then rest assured, you're part of someone else's.

For what it's worth,

The Very Good Dr. Glenn Livingston

The Question I Get Asked Most as a Psychologist

The questions I get asked most as a doctor is "How do you sit with people and hear their problems all day without it affecting you? How do you insulate yourself from their feelings and remain objective?"

The answer is, you don't.

Well, you DO work hard to remain objective. That has to do with paying attention to facts more than feelings, because feelings aren't facts. But you CAN'T insulate yourself from your clients' feelings, because the harder you fight them, the more intense they get, and the more "stuck" inside you they become.

Instead, you must let them PASS THROUGH you, which means you must be very careful about the people you work with, because you are lending them your soul. You must be willing to screen people OUT, even if you need the money. And you must be willing to go through hell with them, if that's where they need to go.

If you choose people who aren't so much complainers as action takers, people who are grateful for the connection and CAPABLE of growth, then it's an extremely rewarding experience. But if you let parasitic people into your practice it can be a very painful experience from which you burn out quickly.

It took me some time to figure this all out.

Nowadays I work on a very specific problem with a very specific, short term solution. Virtually every session is a blessing to both myself and my clients. I watch their feelings of hopelessness and despair dissolve - quickly. It's very uplifting.

But sometimes there are tragedies. Like a woman I only did a simple coaching demonstration with (I'll post it in a few weeks) who had her children taken away from her because she was feeding them raw vegan. That tears your heart out and stays with you. *(Thankfully she IS an action taker - an extremely resilient woman for whom I have the utmost respect. Visit www.HelpZoey.com if you want to help.)*

And you must remember, there are ALSO celebrations. New parents. Business windfalls. Solved marriages. Baby's first steps. When you lend people your soul, you get all the good stuff too!

Overall, I wouldn't trade it for the world. Every day I wake up I pinch myself and ask "Do I really have this job? How in the world did I get so lucky?"

Of course, every now and then I want to get up on top of a clock tower, cover my head in aluminum foil, and scream...

But those days are very few and far between.

I love what I do :-)

PS - The second most frequent question I get asked as a psychologist is "are you analyzing me now?" Dude, NO! It takes a lot of work to analyze someone. You have to put yourself in a very specific state of mind and CONCENTRATE. You must open yourself up to their feelings on the deepest level. So, other than the extent to which EVERYONE is always trying to figure everyone else out... when I'm off duty, I'm really off duty. I just want to watch "Nathan for You" or "Idiocracy" and laugh, play a stupid game, or write a dumb Facebook post. OK?

How I Handle Criticism About Never Binge Again

A take a LOT of heat for my work with Never Binge Again. It used to bother me greatly. Now, I just see it as part of the statistical spread—some love me, some hate me. Que sera' sera'. None of this bothers me anymore, and there are only two essential critiques. Here are the answers:

> **YOU CAN'T RECOVER FROM OVEREATING IF YOU ABDICATE RESPONSIBILITY TO A 'PIG' INSIDE YOU. YOU MUST TAKE RESPONSIBILITY FOR EVERY SINGLE CHOICE YOU HAVE MADE OR YOUR ADDICTION WILL GO ON FOREVER:** This critique can only be made by someone who hasn't genuinely studied Never Binge Again, because NBA is a philosophy of brutal responsibility. We eschew any abdication of power. We ruthlessly root out any notion of being unable to control ourselves. The fact that we choose to organize our minds and identities into very clear constructive vs. destructive thoughts about food makes it MORE possible, not less, to claim responsibility and reject powerlessness.

Furthermore, I don't claim our reptilian brains aren't a part of us any more than I claim our bladders aren't a part of us. I just choose not to give it status as part of my human identity. I prefer to see it as part of my animal nature, which must bow to my human will. The fact I am an animal is not something I deny, but rather a notion I wholeheartedly accept. It is only through this acceptance that I'm able to dominate these primitive drives and make human choices. It is only through this awareness that I'm able to become the person I choose to be.

> **THIS IS JUST A HORRIFIC WAY TO SHAME YOURSELF WHICH WILL MAKE THE PROBLEM WORSE:** Are we

shaming ourselves when we choose to see our bladder as a biological organ which must be subjugated to our will, or would we be shaming ourselves more if we "loved it" and let it express itself wherever it liked? What about our ovaries and/or testicles? Or our road rage reactions?

As a practical matter, self-esteem is related to our ability to habitually make the right choice in the right situation. When we learn to acquire *more* control, we find ourselves with *more* self-esteem, not less. Shame is more associated with feeling powerless and helpless. Listen to some of the demonstration audios at www.NeverBingeAgainPodcast.com if you don't believe me. You'll hear the immediate rise in self-esteem most people feel when we go through a full session! By the way, if you want to learn how to do this with your own clients we also run a training program at www.BecomeAWeightLossCoach.com

Nine Things Most People Didn't Know About Me (Until Now)

Nine things most people never knew about the Very Good Dr. Glenn Livingston:

1. *Money isn't that important to me. I know that's a strange thing to say for someone who focused on business and money for a significant portion of his career, but it's true. I've never been very motivated by material things, and although, except for the 2001-2003 deep debt years, I've always had more than enough for my needs. I've never been "wealthy", but I've always had enough.*

   My real drive is to educate the masses, and to, like, not be yelled at by people I owe money to. But as long as I have love, a roof over my head, a computer with internet, some organic food to eat, a gym to exercise in, am close to the outdoors, and have some project to get all excited about, I'm happy. (Also, I must obsessively watch "Nathan for You." I absolutely, positively, cannot live without that show!)

2. I regularly conduct upside-down business calls. That's not a metaphor...literally, I'm upside down when I'm conducting them. I have an inversion table, which I absolutely love more than I ever loved chocolate. It's great for my sciatica so it's not uncommon for me to grab my iPhone to make some calls and respond to emails while I'm almost completely inverted. I can now even attend a webinar (though not conduct one) in that position.

3. I illegally bugged my father's psychotherapy office when I was 9 years old. He had been on the radio a few times before that, and my mom explained it was because he was good at making people happy when they were sad. I was insatiably curious how he did that and decided I had a really good way to find out. OK, so that was WRONG. I admit that now.

   Thankfully later in life I channeled this drive into more professional aims! But whenever I'm listening to a research interview, sitting with a coaching client, or talking to a patient, I still go back to the exciting intrigue and "figuring out the puzzle" feeling I had when I was 9. *(I hope the NYS statute of limitations is up on that or else now I'm screwed. A 54-year-old man with silver hair and a grey beard wouldn't fare very well in juvenile hall.)*

4. I have a small wart on my right-hand pointer finger. It's been there for at least 40 years. I've seriously thought about getting it removed, but in my childhood each time I removed a wart ONE popped up elsewhere. It's like the wart-monster in my body says "just let me

have ONE and I'll leave you alone!" So, I've always been scared to remove it and have it end up god-knows where. There's an analogy in overeating recovery... sometimes there's a small wart you decide to put up with. Maybe your weight is a few pounds above super-model status. Maybe there's a meal which you less than thoroughly enjoy. (*If you don't like a meal by the way, there's always another one coming in a few hours*). Or maybe it's having to put up with a modestly uncom-fortable craving without indulging because you forgot to pack lunch.

5. In my early 30s, I had a patient who told me she was going to get up from her chair and bitch slap me if I didn't answer her question. After scrambling in my head to remember what the textbooks said I should do in that situation, I just went ahead and answered it. She became one of the best patients I ever had. I remem-ber this in food recovery sometimes: You can't plan for everything no matter how much shopping, prepping, and cooking you do. At some point you're going to get bitch slapped if you don't improvise. Figure out the rules for those times and just live with it.

6. When my dog Zachary got tired, he would fall asleep with his tongue out. (Me too)

7. Just after graduate school I seriously entertained the possibility of bolting from both my psychology and marketing research careers to compose jazz music for the piano. I submitted several tapes to Polygram and got all the way to a meeting with the President. Thank God I didn't go through with it however, because al-though I was talented, I really didn't have the training or experience to shape that talent into a professional career. Anyway, here's a little recording from 2006 or

so (when I was still a little fat) playing something I wrote, just in case you feel like listening. Plenty of mistakes in this – oh well.
https://youtu.be/bfGxbHBx9EU

8. Once, when I was 7, I got really mad at my sister and punched a hole in the wall in her bedroom. Rather than getting upset, she asked me why I never told her I was Superman. I just went with it. I think she still thinks that. My sister is the blonde in the video above

9. I can't get contact lenses in my eyes. Seriously, I've spent hours with very gentle eye professionals who swear they're going to be the one to fix the problem, but whatever they do, my eye closes when the stupid contact is an inch away. Oh well, I guess it's good for us all to know our weaknesses. *"If you spend too much time trying to strengthen your weaknesses, you'll wind up weakening your strengths!"*

My Favorite Quotes of All Time

➢ "A life of discipline is better than a life of regret" – Jim Rohn

➢ "You can have *anything* you want but you can't have *everything* you want" – Peter McWilliams

➢ "Life is never made unbearable by circumstances, only by lack of meaning and purpose" – Victor Frankl

➢ "It takes constant repetition to force alien concepts on reluctant minds" – Sigmund Freud

➢ "Darkness cannot drive out darkness: only light can do that. Hate cannot drive out hate: only love can do that" – Martin Luther King

➢ "Success is not final, failure is not fatal: it is the courage to continue that counts" – Winston Churchill

➢ "Everyone thinks of changing the world but nobody thinks of changing himself." – Leo Tolstoy

➢ "Success is going from failure to failure without losing your enthusiasm." – Winston Churchill

➢ "Words are singularly the most powerful force available to humanity. We can choose to use this force constructively with words of encouragement, or destructively using words of despair. Words have energy and power with the ability to help, to heal, to hinder, to hurt, to humiliate, and to humble" – Yehuda Berg

➢ "The best way out is always through." – Robert Frost

➢ "To handle yourself, use your head. To handle others, use your heart." – Elanor Roosevelt

➢ "People don't care how much you know until they know how much you care." – Theodore Roosevelt

➢ "The most common way people give up their power is by thinking they don't have any." – Alice Walker

➢ "Nothing will work unless you do." – Maya Angelou

➢ "Say what you mean but don't say it mean" - Unknown

APPENDIX C - UNUSUAL BOOKS THAT HAVE INFLUENCED ME

There are some lesser-known books from my psychology background which have direct implications for overcoming binge eating, and which had a significant influence on my thinking as I developed Never Binge Again:

> **"Making Things Better by Making Them Worse"**: (Alan Fay). Why? Because people tend to become constrained by their own thoughts. It's VERY easy to become myopic and stuck in your own head while you're looking for the "right" answer to overcome a particular rationalization your Reptilian Brain offers, but it turns out, one of the best ways to find the right answer is to look for the wrong one! This is a psychological treatise about paradoxical thinking and paradoxical interventions, not a book on binge eating, but it's very valuable, nonetheless. For example, if you're having trouble dealing with a particular Pig Squeal (rationalization for eating off your diet) try writing down a list of twenty way you could make the Squeal even MORE appealing. Don't restrain yourself – and don't use any of them either – just write! Once they're all on the table, read them over a few times and then come up with a list of at least 10

reasons the Squeal is nonsensical.

> **"Rational Recovery" (Jack Trimpey).** Why? This is the book which convinced me of the dual-minded nature of food addiction *(You vs. the Reptilian Brain or your "Pig")*, indeed, of any addiction. I had to evolve this idea and make a number of very significant modifications to get it to work with food *(Trimpey built it largely for drugs and alcohol)* but it was a seminal experience for me and radically altered my thinking. Without it I would've taken many more years to come to the conclusions I did, I'm sure. Rational Recovery will also sensitize you to the fact that an entire industry, in fact an entire country can be factually wrong, yet get dramatically swept away with a philosophy or "truth". The vast majority of the world now supports the 12-step model of recovery, yet there's really NO scientific evidence for this model. It succeeds due to its viral nature. There are indeed valuable things going on in the recovery movement... but the point here is that everyone has assumed evidence which doesn't exist.

> **"Cats Cradle" (Kurt Vonnegut).** Why? A LOT of people comment that when they listen to the hundreds of podcasts I put out with coaching demonstrations *(www.NeverBingeAgainPodcast.com)*, they are constantly amazed at how accepting and non-judgmental I am. Well, believe it or not this book helped me develop that ability. The moral of Cats Cradle is "People should live by the myths which make them happy and kind, regardless of their truth". This had profound implications for how I learned to be tolerant of other people's thoughts and feelings, even when I vehemently disagree with them. Everyone has fantasies and wishes about IDEALIZED solutions to their problems, and corresponding REALITIES which grate against these. Determining how, when, and why to give people the truth without losing their interest is an art form. Think about this

while you read this very entertaining, fast moving short story

> **A Journey Through Your Childhood (Christopher Biffle):** Why? Because being able to fully bear your soul requires you know the full essence of your being, including (and perhaps especially) the powerful stories which have made you who you are. The questions and exercises in this book have helped me to much better know myself.

> **Neurotic Styles (David Shapiro):** Why? Neurosis pervades all factions of society today, and you'll definitely be dealing with neurotic people if you want to participate in life, and participating in life is what you'll be doing when you stop overeating! No one explains neurosis better for the lay public than David Shapiro. Even 30 years later, this is still one of my favorites.

LEGAL: "Honey Comb" is a registered trademark of Post Cereals (Kraft Foods). "Pop-Tarts", "Frosted Flakes", and "Sugar Pops" are registered trademarks of Kellogg Company. "Cocoa Puffs", "Frankenberry", and "Lucky Charms" are registered trademarks of General Mills. "Spirograph" is a registered trademark of Hasbro. "Etch a Sketch" is a registered trademark of Spin Master. "Chutes and Ladders" is a registered trademark of Milton Bradley.

LEGAL: Tootsie Pops™ and Tootsie Roll™ are registered trademarks of Tootsie Roll Industries and WorldPantry.com, Inc. Doublemint is a registered trademark of Wrigley corporation.

© Psy Tech Inc. and Never Ever Again, Inc. All Rights Reserved

Made in the USA
Monee, IL
21 March 2023

30281492R00100